John Carroll

Project 2010

in
easy steps

In easy steps is an imprint of In Easy Steps Limited
Southfield Road · Southam
Warwickshire CV47 0FB · United Kingdom
www.ineasysteps.com

Notice of Liability
Every effort has been made to ensure that this book contains accurate
and current information. However, In Easy Steps Limited and the
author shall not be liable for any loss or damage suffered by readers
as a result of any information contained herein.

Trademarks
All trademarks are acknowledged as belonging to their respective
companies.

In Easy Steps Limited supports The Forest Stewardship Council (FSC),
the leading international forest certification organisation. All our titles
that are printed on Greenpeace approved FSC certified paper carry the
FSC logo.

MIX
Paper from
responsible sources
FSC C020837

FSC
www.fsc.org

Printed and bound in the United Kingdom

ISBN 978-1-84078-397-1

Contents

1 The Basics — 7

Introduction	8
Project Management	9
What's New?	10
Version Comparison	12
The Gantt Chart	14
Getting Help	15
Summary	16

2 User Interface — 17

User Interface	18
File	20
Task	22
Resource	24
Project	26
View	28
Format	30
Quick Access Toolbar	32
Summary	34

3 Managing your Project — 35

A 4-Step Approach	36
Step 1: Define the Objectives	37
Step 2: Develop the Plan	38
Tasks and Deliverables	39
Milestones	40
Step 3: Carry it Out	41
Saving Your Project	42
Step 4: Hand it Over	43
Summary	44

4 Working with Tasks — 45

Creating a Task	46
Task Duration	48
Adding Tasks	49
Task Dependencies	50
Linking Tasks	51
Unlinking Tasks	52
Changing Dependencies	53
Moving a Task	54
Deleting a Task	55
Task Form	56

Project Milestones 57
Recurring Tasks 58
Work Effort v Duration 59
Summary 60

5 Adding Structure 61

Project Structure 62
Summary Tasks 63
Project Stages 64
Changing the Timescale 66
Outline Numbering 67
Subtasks 68
Summary 70

6 More About Tasks 71

Lag Time and Lead Time 72
Task Inspector 74
Task Notes 75
Deadline Dates 76
Moving Around 77
Critical Path 78
Critical Tasks 79
Splitting Tasks 80
Moving Linked Tasks 81
Summary 82

7 Resources 83

Resource Sheet 84
Resource Information 85
Material & Cost Resources 86
Resource Notes 87
Assigning Resources 88
Multiple Resources 89
Team Planner 90
Timeline 92
Summary 94

8 Project Costs 95

Project Costs 96
Resource Costs 97
Fixed Costs 98
Variable Resource Costs 99
Cost Rate Tables 100
Applying Resource Rates 101
Cost Resources 102
Summary 104

9   Project Calendars   105

Calendars	106
Project Defaults	108
Standard Calendar	109
New Base Calendar	110
Assigning a Calendar	111
Task Calendar	112
Resource Calendar	114
Summary	116

10   Project Scheduling   117

User Controlled Scheduling	118
Automatic Scheduling	119
Fixed Unit Tasks	120
Fixed Duration Tasks	121
Fixed Work Tasks	122
Resource Contouring	123
Task Contouring	124
Setting a Baseline	126
Interim Plans	127
Clearing a Baseline	128
Backward-Scheduling	129
Summary	130

11   Conflicts and Constraints   131

Resource Conflicts	132
Resource Leveling	134
Manual Adjustments	136
Task Constraints	138
Applying Constraints	139
Constraint Conflicts	140
Viewing Constraints	141
Calculate Project	142
Move Project	143
Summary	144

12   Viewing Data   145

Views	146
Tables	147
Grouping	148
Fiscal Year	150
Filters	151
AutoFilter	152
Filter Criteria	153
Filter by Resource	154
Sorting	155
Highlight Filters	156
Fonts and Highlighting	157
Custom Fields	158
Graphic Indicators	159
Summary	160

13 Reports 161

Printing a View 162
Headers and Footers 163
Previewing Reports 164
Page Setup and Scaling 165
Printing Reports 166
Visual Reports 167
Copy Picture 168
Project Collaboration 169
Enhanced Copy/Paste 170
Summary 172

14 Tracking Progress 173

Progress Tracking 174
Completed Work 175
Part Completed Work 176
Percentage Completed 177
Duration Completed 178
Entering Costs 179
Updating as Scheduled 180
Actual v Baseline 181
Tracking Gantt Chart 182
Budget Tracking 183
Project Statistics 184
Progress Lines 185
Summary 186

Index 187

1 The Basics

*This chapter introduces
Microsoft Project 2010 and
explains how it can help you
manage your projects.*

8   Introduction

9   Project Management

10   What's New?

12   Version Comparison

14   The Gantt Chart

15   Getting Help

16   Summary

Introduction

Microsoft Project 2010 (whether you have the Project Standard or Project Professional version) is a great project management tool. Managing projects can be a complex activity but, with the help of Project, you can plan, schedule, track and communicate the progress of your project, so that you stay in control of it.

The Standard and Professional versions of Project are very similar, when used in "stand-alone" mode, and this book covers both. In addition to the functionality of the Standard version, the Professional version allows you to collaborate and share information with other Project users in your organization, through the use of Project Server and SharePoint (companion products).

Whether your project is a simple, short-term one (such as arranging a company event) or a more complex project (like launching a new product), Project 2010 can help you stay in control of it.

Project 2010 Features

Used as a planning tool, Project can produce some great looking charts and diagrams to help you plan your project. But Project can do a lot more besides:

- It can help you to understand, develop and manage project plans and schedules

- It can produce a critical path analysis to identify the areas you will need to keep a close track on progress

- It can identify if you have too much work allocated to any one person

- It can schedule facilities, such as meeting rooms and equipment for you

- It can help you to understand and control project budgets and costs

- It can keep track of public holidays and team members' vacations

- It can help you build professional looking reports to communicate and present project information in an effective and understandable way

Beware

The examples and illustrations in this book are from Project 2010. If you are using an earlier version, many features will look very different and may not be available.

Hot tip

Project 2007 in easy steps covers all the earlier versions, from Project 98 onwards.

Project Management

Successful project management is about completing a project on time, within budget, and with the needs of the business fully met. While this is easy to say, a large percentage of projects fail. The most commonly quoted figure is around half of all projects, although, depending on how you define failure, it could be as little as 25% (total failure) or as much as 75% (failed or seriously challenged).

Whichever way you look at it, only around one quarter of projects end up as fully successful (i.e. completed on time, within budget, and with the required scope). In order to get most projects completed, corners have to be cut, but things still seem to take longer than expected. As a further result, costs inevitably seem to increase.

Successful Projects

It doesn't have to be that way. We know how to ensure projects are successful, it's not rocket science, it's just plain common sense. Throughout this book, you will find some basic project management concepts that have been proved in practice. Follow these concepts and advice to ensure that your project will be successful.

Microsoft Project

Microsoft Project is a great product that will help you plan, organize and control your project. It won't carry it out for you (you still have to do that yourself), but what it will do is help you to control and complete it successfully.

Hot tip

Project Management in easy steps is a companion book and covers project management in much more detail.

What's New?

There are a number of significant changes and enhancements in Project 2010, which are noted, where relevant, throughout the book. The key new features and functionality are:

User Interface

Microsoft has introduced the Fluent User Interface (or ribbon) to replace the traditional toolbars and buttons found on earlier versions of Project, up to Project 2007.

Enhanced Tables

The Tables in Project 2010 now act more like Excel tables, with the following significant enhancements:

- Columns can be added dynamically, by entering data without the need to select data type

- Simplified data entry with auto-complete and enhanced color and text formatting options

- Automatic text wrap adjusts the row height to display the full task name

- Filter available on each column, to quickly find data and analyze results

- Improved copy and paste functionality, to share data and formatting between Project and other applications

Beware

Please note that the dates illustrated in this book are in MM/DD/YY format.

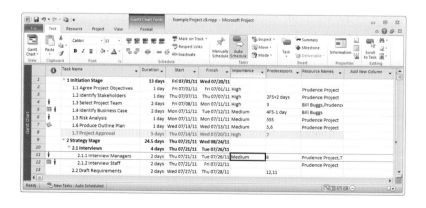

User-Controlled Scheduling

In previous versions of Project, tasks would automatically be scheduled to begin either on the current date (if the task had no predecessor) or directly after any preceding tasks are completed. In Project 2010, the user has far more control over scheduling:

- You can manually schedule tasks with any (or no) information you currently have, or allow Project to schedule tasks automatically with calculated start and end dates

- Project will alert you of any scheduling concerns with squiggly underlines

- Task Inspector will provide more details and assist you in solving problems

- You can also create high-level schedules using top-down summary tasks

Timeline View

This new function allows you to share a simple visual timeline with all project stakeholders. The timeline can be tailored and customized to effectively display the key information and dates relevant to each group.

Version Comparison

Project Standard

In addition to the new features listed in the preceding topic, Project Standard 2010 contains a number of enhancements from the previous version (Project Standard 2007):

- Hovering over a command brings up detailed Tool Tips, as illustrated below

- The new navigation ribbon (replacing the menu bar) can be customized

- Tools, templates and program options are all now accessible in the File view

- Placeholder text can be entered in date and other data fields to allow for later completion, as illustrated below

- Tasks can be defined as active or inactive and the impact of this on the schedule can be reviewed

- The new Task Inspector function provides information on dealing with overallocated resources or scheduling problems

- Enhancements to the copy and paste functionality means that outline levels and formatting information can now be retained

- User-controlled scheduling allows for greater flexibility than automatic scheduling on its own

- Resource levelling and resource substitution functionality has been enhanced to provide support for additional techniques

- PDF and XPS file save formats are now supported

Project Professional

In addition to the new and enhanced features in Project Standard, the Professional version of Project 2010 contains the following additional functionality:

Team Planner

Providing visual dragging and dropping of assignment changes, to deal with work overload, as illustrated below

Enhanced Collaboration

Integration allows project schedules to be published and shared, with SharePoint. Synchronization of schedules between Project Professional and SharePoint task lists can be performed, so that changes can be made by team members and reflected back into the Project schedule.

The Gantt Chart

The first thing you see when you open or create a new project is the Gantt chart. It is the default view, and with good reason. The Gantt chart is probably the most widely used and most useful project management tool.

Summary Level

They say that every picture tells a thousand words, and this is the key picture in your project:

At the summary-level (as illustrated above), you can view the whole project on one screen or sheet of paper. The Gantt chart represents the most frequently used way of representing a project graphically and is particularly useful for senior management in its rolled-up summary form (as above).

Detailed Level

At the more detailed level (as illustrated below), the Gantt chart is typically used by the project manager to communicate with the project team, and to track project progress, by task, on a day-to-day basis.

In addition to letting you view the project schedule at the strategic (high-level) and operational (detailed-level), the Gantt chart view also allows you to insert and edit tasks, and allocate the people and other resources to work on the tasks. You can set milestones and deadlines, and generally keep track of your project and the resources working on it.

Getting Help

Getting extensive help in Project is fairly straight forward, and is only a couple of clicks or the press of the F1 function key away:

1 Select Help from the File ribbon for the full range of options, as illustrated below

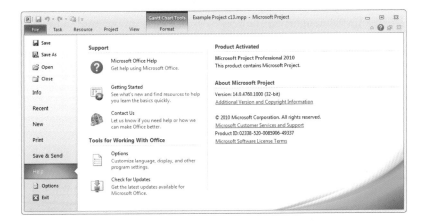

2 Click on Office Help (or use the F1 function key) to open the Project Help dialog box

3 Select the required category and sub-category and the required help text will be displayed, or type a query and click Search

4 Click on Show Table of Contents to bring up the full, expandable table of contents in a side pane, as illustrated right

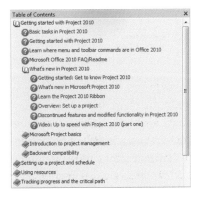

5 Click it again to hide the table of contents

Summary

- Microsoft Project can help you to plan and schedule your project, allocate tasks, and track progress and costs

- One thing Project can't do for you is manage the actual work of your project. Around 50% of projects fail for reasons that are known and understood. This book includes some proven project management concepts to help you make sure your project is a success

- Project 2010 introduces the Fluent User Interface (or ribbon), bringing Project into line with the rest of the Microsoft Office suite

- Enhanced Tables now act more like Excel tables with: dynamic column addition, simplified data entry, automatic text wrapping, column filter, and improved copy and paste functionality

- User Controlled Scheduling allows you to choose whether to manually schedule tasks or to let Project schedule them for you automatically

- Project can now alert you to any scheduling concerns and, with an improved Task Inspector function, these can easily be rectified

- The new Timeline View allows you to communicate a high level view of the project through other Office applications

- Project Standard has a number of further enhancements and improvements, while Project Professional also adds Team Planner (with visual drag and drop of tasks and resources) and Enhanced Collaboration (allowing you to publish, share and synchronize information between Project and SharePoint)

- The Gantt chart is the most useful view in Project, and the one in which you will probably choose to do most of your work. At the summary level it is great for communicating strategically, while at the detailed level it is great for working with the team on a day to day basis

- Getting help is only a click away, or you can use the F1 to go direct to the Project Help dialog box and full help contents

2 User Interface

The new User Interface (or ribbon) replaces the old menu and button toolbars. It provides a different method for accessing menu items that is compatible with the other Office 2010 applications.

18   User Interface

20   File

22   Task

24   Resource

26   Project

28   View

30   Format

32   Quick Access Toolbar

34   Summary

User Interface

The Fluent User Interface (or ribbon) replaces the traditional drop-down menu and button toolbars Project used up to Project 2007. It now brings Project 2010 into line with other Microsoft Office applications. The user interface consists of a series of tabs, each of which invokes a ribbon containing different menu items and program functions.

Hot tip

Full details of all these views and functions are contained in the rest of this chapter.

As can be seen above, there are six tabs: File, Task, Resource, Project, View and Format. These effectively replace the traditional Windows Menu items.

There is also a group of icons at the top left, this is the new Quick Access Toolbar (covered on page 32). Top right are the window size, close and help functions, plus the show/hide ribbon.

Finally, upper-center is an indicator of the current tools being displayed, in this case Gantt Chart Tools (indicating that we are in Gantt Chart view), together with the file name (Project1) and file type (Microsoft Project).

File

When the File tab is selected, by clicking on it, the file view is displayed. This is different from the other views tabs (as can be seen from the illustration below) and is covered on page 20.

Task

This is the default ribbon when working in a Gantt Chart, and it is covered on page 22:

Resource

This ribbon is used to assign and manage resources on the project, and is covered on page 24:

Project

This ribbon is used to set up basic project and status information, and is covered on page 26:

View

This ribbon is used to control views, data, sorting and filters, and is covered on page 28.

Format

This ribbon is used to control the format of charts and data in tables, and is covered on page 30:

File

When the File Tab is selected, the following File view (strictly speaking it is not a ribbon) is displayed:

In addition to the normal File operations (Save, Save As, Open and Close) down the left-hand side, there are also a further series of Tabs (Info, Recent, New, Print, Save & Send and Help) together with Options and Exit. The Info Tab (as selected above) brings up the options for managing accounts on Project Server (a companion product), Organizing the Global Template and updating the Project Information.

Recent

The Recent Tab on the left-hand side brings up a list of recently used files. Clicking on any of them will open the selected file.

New

The New Tab brings up the following options for selecting a template or starting with a blank project:

Print

The Print Tab brings up the standard print options, together with a preview of what will be printed.

Save & Send

The Save & Send Tab brings up the sharing options: Send as Attachment, Synchronize with task list, Save to SharePoint, Save Project as File and Create PDF/XPS Document

Help

The Help Tab brings up the Help options, which are covered in the previous chapter, on page 15.

Task

When the Task tab on the user interface is selected, the following task ribbon is displayed:

The ribbon is divided into eight groups, each containing one or more functions. Working from left to right, these are:

View

This group contains one function, the Gantt Chart, which can be selected to switch back to Gantt Chart view at any time. There is also a down arrow beneath it, which produces a drop-down list of the 12 built in views (as illustrated on the right). It also has More Views at the bottom, which brings up the full list of all 27 available views.

Clipboard

This group includes the cut, copy, paste and format painter functions. Copy includes copy picture and Paste includes paste special and paste as a hyperlink.

Font

This group contains the font attributes, including background color. There is also a link (at the bottom right of the group) to the Font dialog box (as illustrated on the right), where all font attributes can be set.

Schedule

This group includes the task progress functions: 0%, 25%, 50%, 75% and 100%, together with mark on track (which marks the task as completed up to the current date).

The group also includes functions for indent, outdent, split task, link and unlink tasks, respect links and make task active or inactive. Making a task inactive means it no longer affects the schedule or resources.

Tasks

This group contains functions to set a task to manually or automatically schedule. Where a task is automatically scheduled, Project will set it to start on the current date or immediately after any predecessor tasks are completed. Where a task is manually scheduled, you will need to enter the start date and duration.

The group also contains functions to open task inspector (which provides information on scheduling details and any issues) and move a task. Finally, it includes a mode function, which allows you to select whether all new tasks will be manually or automatically scheduled. Selecting this function will not change any existing tasks, but they can still be changed individually.

Insert

The insert group allows you to insert new tasks, summary tasks, milestones and a link to deliverables and dependencies (which will be greyed out unless you are linked to Project Server, (a companion product).

There is a down arrow beneath the insert new task button that brings up further insert options, as illustrated on the right.

Properties

This group contains task information, which brings up the task information dialog box (as illustrated below). The group also contains task note, task details and add task to timeline functions.

Editing

The final group includes scroll to task, find/replace text, clear cell content (or formatting) and fill. Fill provides a function that copies a value from one cell into one or more adjacent cells.

Resource

When the Resource tab on the user interface is selected, the following resource ribbon is displayed:

The ribbon is divided into five groups, each of which contains one or more functions. Working from left to right, the groups are:

View

This contains one function, the team planner view, to switch to that view (only available in Project Professional). There is also a down arrow beneath it, which can be selected to produce a drop-down list of the 12 built in views and a More Views option that produces the full list of all 27 available views.

Assignments

This group contains three functions: assign resources, resource pool and substitute resources. If the assign resources button is selected, the assign resource dialog box opens (as illustrated on the right) and displays the available resources for the project.

If the resource pool is selected, the share resources dialog box opens (as illustrated on the right) and allows resources to be shared over several projects, by creating a common resource pool. This allows control of resources working on more than one project.

Substitute resources will be greyed out unless you are connected to Project Server (a companion product).

Insert

This group consists of just one function: add resources and, if selected, it will display the options illustrated on the right. Selecting work resources will allow you to type in the new resource name. Alternatively, you can select people from Active Directory or an Outlook address book.

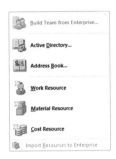

Properties

This group consists of three functions: information, notes and details. Selecting information will bring up the resource information dialog box, as illustrated below.

This allows information about the selected resource to be edited, the change working time function (right hand side above) allows changes to working days and hours and non-working time, such as vacations, to be input.

The notes function allows text notes to be attached to a resource, while the details function shows additional details for the selected resource.

Level

The final group contains six functions: level selection, level resource, level all, levelling options, clear levelling and go to next overallocation. The levelling process is a technique to deal with overallocations (where a resource has too much work allocated to them) and is covered in chapter 11.

Project

When the Project tab on the user interface is selected, the following project ribbon is displayed:

The ribbon is divided into six groups, each of which contains one or more functions. Working from left to right, the groups are:

Insert

This group contains one function: insert subproject. This feature allows you to insert an existing project file into the current project, as a subproject.

Properties

This group contains five functions: project information, custom fields, links between projects, WBS (work breakdown structure) and change working time. Project information is where you can set the start date and various other attributes for the project.

Custom fields allows you to create your own fields and assign attributes (such as graphic indicators) to them. Links between projects display any external dependencies between the tasks in the current project and tasks in other projects. WBS allows you to define or modify your own work breakdown structure and also renumber tasks. Change working time allows you to set the overall working time and working/nonworking days for the project, or for individual resources and tasks.

Schedule

This group contains three functions: calculate project, set baseline and move project. Calculate project will re-schedule the project following any changes. It is only necessary if you have turned off calculation in the project options dialog box (see chapter 11). Set baseline will bring up the set baseline dialog box, which will allow you to set a number of baselines and interim plans for the whole project or a range of selected tasks. It also has an option to clear a baseline or interim plan. Move project allows you to change the project start date and reschedule the project on this basis. It also has the option to reschedule deadline dates, if required.

Status

This group contains three functions: status date, update project and synchronize (sync) to protected actuals. Status date allows you to change the effective reporting date. This is the date that then appears on reports and is used for calculation purposes. If it is not changed, it defaults to the current date. Update project brings up the update project dialog box, which allows you to update progress on the entire project or selected tasks. Sync to protected actuals is a Project Server function that will be greyed out if you are not connected to Project Server (a companion product). It updates the actual data in the current project with the values held on the project server.

Reports

This group contains three functions: visual reports, reports and compare projects. Visual reports allows you to view dates from the project in pivot tables in Excel, and pivot diagrams in Visio. Visual reports are covered in chapter 13.

Reports brings up the reports dialog box (as illustrated right). This contains five groups of predefined reports (22 reports in all) and custom reports, allowing you to create new reports.

Compare projects will produce an analysis of two versions of the same project, identifying any differences, such as new tasks added or items edited.

Proofing

The final group contains just one function, to check the spelling of the text fields in the project.

View

When the View tab on the user interface is selected, the following view ribbon is displayed:

The ribbon is divided into seven groups, each of which contains one or more functions. Working across from left to right, these groups are:

Task Views

This group contains five functions: Gantt chart, task usage, network diagram, calendar and other views. Gantt chart will bring up the default Gantt chart view. Task usage lists the tasks, with the resources assigned to them and the work scheduled. Network diagram gives an alternative to the Gantt chart, which has a box representing each task linked by dependency lines.

Calendar displays a monthly or weekly calendar, with the project tasks displayed on the dates where they are scheduled. Other views lists the remaining, built in, task views together with a more views option (which brings up all 27 available views).

Resource Views

This group contains four functions: team planner, resource usage, resource sheet and other views. Team planner (only available in Project Professional) provides a graphical schedule, which allows tasks to be dragged and dropped between resources, to assign or reassign them. Resource usage lists resources with the tasks assigned to them and when they are scheduled. Resource sheet lists all the resources with their full details. Other views lists the remaining built in resource views, together with a more views option (which brings up all 27 available views).

Data

This group contains six functions: sort, outline, tables, highlight, filter and group. Sort brings up a list of sort options (start date, finish date, priority, cost or ID) and a sort by option, which brings up the sort dialog box. This enables a sort by multiple fields with ascending/descending options and the ability to renumber tasks or retain the existing outline structure.

Outline allows you to show or hide subtasks or select any outline level. Tables allows you to select from built in tables appropriate to the current view or more tables, which allows you to select from the full list of 17 task tables and 10 resource tables. Highlight allows you to select from a range of built in highlight options (such as late tasks) or to select from a full range of all available options, including ranges. Group lets you group data by selecting from a range of built in options or from a full list of available options.

Zoom

This group contains four functions: timescale, zoom, whole project and selected tasks. Timescale allows you to select the granularity for the chart side of the view (e.g. days, weeks, months) or to use the timescale dialog box to customize the timescale and the way in which non-working time is displayed.

Zoom allows you to zoom in or out of the current chart view. Whole project brings the whole project into view. Selected tasks is a useful feature that allows you to select one or more tasks on the table side and bring them into view on the chart side.

Split View

This group consists of two functions: timeline and details. If timeline is selected, the timeline view is displayed above the Gantt chart. If details are selected, the task form is displayed underneath the Gantt chart. Selecting either of these options will deselect the other option. Once either option is selected, a drop down menu becomes available alongside it, so that any other available view can be selected to replace the default.

Window

This group consists of four functions: new window, switch windows, arrange all or hide window. New window opens another view of the current project, and you can select from a drop down list of available views. Switch window lets you switch between open windows. Arrange all will tile all open windows side by side. Hide window will hide the currently selected window.

Macros

This group allows you to view or record macros, edit visual basic or define macro security. These are all advanced functions outside the scope of this book.

Format

When the Format tab on the user interface is selected, the format ribbon that will be displayed will depend on the current view displayed. If the Gantt chart view is currently displayed, the following format ribbon will be displayed:

If the task usage view is selected, the following format ribbon will be displayed:

The following groups appear in these two format views, and many of the other format views as well:

Format

This group will contain some or all text styles, gridlines and layout. Text styles brings up the text styles dialog box, enabling the text style, size and color to be set. Gridlines enables the gridlines and progress lines on a chart to be defined. Layout enables the size and shape of bars and link lines to be defined.

Columns

This group will contain insert column, left/center/right justify, wrap text, column settings and custom fields. Insert column displays a selection list for all the standard data fields that can be inserted, or the option to create a custom field. Justify will format the text in the selected columns. Wrap text will allow a long task name to be displayed by increasing the depth of the row. Column settings allows columns to be hidden, text wrapped and formatted in detail. Custom fields brings up the custom fields dialog box, allowing custom fields to be added and defined.

Bar Styles

This group will contain format, critical tasks, slack, late tasks, baseline and slippage. Format allows you to change the shape and color of a bar for a selected task, or the style for all tasks.

Selecting critical will turn all critical task bars red. Selecting slack will insert a line to show any slack (float) time. Selecting late tasks will turn any late tasks bars black. Baseline will display a bar for the baseline (if set) under the task bar. Slippage will display a line in front of the task bar showing slippage from the baseline.

Gantt Chart Style

This group will contain a selection of different colored styles and a link (bottom right) to the bar styles dialog box. Selecting any of the styles will change the color of the bars on the Gantt chart. The bar styles dialog box gives much more detailed control over the appearance and color of bars.

Show/Hide

This group contains outline number, project summary task and summary tasks. Selecting outline number will display a number in front of each task name in the format, 1.1.1 representing the outline level of the task. Selecting project summary task will insert a top-level task at top of the sheet, with a summary bar on the chart. Selecting summary tasks will display summary tasks. If it is not selected, summary tasks will not be displayed.

Drawings

This group contains only one function: drawing, which enables you to insert or update a drawing on the chart. Selecting this produces a pop up selection of drawing shapes and tools.

Details

This group will contain: work, actual work, cumulative work, baseline work, cost, actual cost and add details. Selecting any of the first six will add that information as another line under each task and resource. Add details opens a detailed dialog box allowing you to select to show or hide any information and also format it.

Assignment

This group contains two functions: information (which brings up the assignment information dialog box) and notes (which brings up the notes dialog box). These allow you to amend the details of the assignment and to add notes.

The other views will have similar format information to these, together with any view specific formatting options.

Quick Access Toolbar

The quick access toolbar is displayed in the top left hand corner of the Project window, as illustrated below:

Project

In the illustration above, there are five icons. The first of these is the Project icon, selecting this will produce the drop down menu (as illustrated on the right). These are the standard window functions and, strictly speaking, are not part of the quick access toolbar.

Save

The next icon (representing a floppy disk) in the quick access toolbar is the save icon. Selecting this saves the current project.

Undo

The curly left arrow is the undo icon. When it is active (not greyed out), selecting it will undo the last change made to the project.

Redo

The curly right arrow is the redo icon. Selecting it will redo a change after it has been undone.

Customize Toolbar

The final icon is a drop down arrow, this brings up the customize quick access toolbar (as illustrated on the right).

Any of the selected items (those with ticks beside them) can be deselected, and any of the other listed items can be selected to add them to the quick access toolbar. More commands will bring up a dialog box, as illustrated at the top of the page opposite.

Changes can then be made to the Quick Access Toolbar, in the dialog box illustrated above, as follows:

1 Select any functions to be removed from the Quick Access Toolbar in the right hand pane, and then click the Remove button in the middle

2 Select any functions from the popular commands in the left hand pane to be added and click the Add button in the middle (Copy Picture has just been added, in the illustration above)

3 To move any function up or down the list, select it in the right hand pane and click the up or down arrows on the right hand side

4 Click OK at the bottom to save the changes

Note that additional functions are available if the drop down arrow beside popular commands, at the top, is selected.

Summary

- The Fluent User Interface (ribbon) has now replaced the drop-down menu and button toolbars from previous versions of Project. It contains six tabs to bring up the file, task, resource, project, view and format ribbons, together with a quick access toolbar

- File has the usual save and save as functions as well as options for selecting recently used files to open, creating a new file from a template, printing the current view, save & send (sharing options) and help

- Task has options for selecting the view, clipboard (cut, copy and paste), font changes, updating progress, scheduling options (manually or automatically scheduling tasks) and options for finding and editing content and formatting

- Resource has options for selecting the view, assigning resources to tasks, setting up a resource pool, adding and editing resources and levelling (the process of reallocating work to remove overloads)

- Project has options for inserting a subproject, setting the start date and other attributes for the project, defining custom fields, managing links between projects, defining a work breakdown structure, changing working time, scheduling, setting baselines, updating project status, producing visual and printed reports and spell checking

- View has options for selecting any of the 27 available views, sorting, grouping and filtering data, showing or hiding sub-tasks and summary tasks, showing a timeline or task details, arranging windows and macros

- Format has options for defining text styles, grid lines and layout, formatting columns and wrapping text, changing bar and chart styles, showing/hiding outline numbers, summary tasks and the project summary task, creating and editing drawings, selecting details to be displayed and editing assignment details

- Quick Access Toolbar is visible in all views, and it provides quick access to frequently used commands. It can be customized, to add or remove commands

3 Managing your Project

This chapter introduces a structured approach to managing a project and explores some of the ways Project 2010 can help you manage your project.

36 A 4-Step Approach

37 Step 1: Define the Objectives

38 Step 2: Develop the Plan

39 Tasks and Deliverables

40 Milestones

41 Step 3: Carry it Out

42 Saving Your Project

43 Step 4: Hand it Over

44 Summary

A 4-Step Approach

Project management is the management of change.

In order to manage change, and, therefore, manage your project, you will need to perform a number of tasks. But, rather than just jumping straight in and starting to define these tasks, it is a good idea to take a more structured approach to a project.

These four steps will give you just that:

1 Define the Objectives: start by identifying what you are trying to achieve, the aims or goals of the project and where you want to get to by the end of the project

2 Develop the Plan: once you have defined the objectives, you can then plan how you are going to go about achieving them

3 Carry it Out: once you have planned the project, you will need to carry it out or manage it until the project is completed and the objectives have been achieved

4 Hand it Over: once you have completed the project, you have done your job as project manager and it is time to hand over the results of the project to whoever will be managing the process or system going forward

Unfortunately, a lot of projects seem to start at Step 3! It's what's known as the "Just Do It" school of management. But, even if you start your project at Step 2, what's the use of a plan if you don't know where you are going? So start at the beginning.

Interestingly, the difficult step for some project managers is the last one. They find it difficult to let go.

The project manager's job is to implement change. Once that change has been implemented, their role as project manager is completed. The new, changed state becomes a production process, and that requires production (rather than project) management.

In the remainder of this chapter, we will expand on each of these four steps and look at what is involved, starting with Step 1: Defining the Objectives.

Step 1: Define the Objectives

The first step in any project is to define the objectives. You need to do this in order to be able to:

- Make sure you have identified the right target

- Focus the other members of the project team on what the project is about

- Create team commitment to, and agreement about, the project objectives

- Ensure that you involve all interested parties in achieving a successful project outcome

SMART Objectives

When you set out to define your objectives, there is a useful acronym to remember: SMART. It stands for Strategic, Measurable, Agreed, Realistic and Timed.

Strategic

The objectives must address some strategic business purpose or need. If they do not, does the project really matter to the business and, if not, why carry it out?

Measurable

If you can't measure project achievement, how will you know if you've achieved anything?

Agreed

If the rest of the business, and the rest of the project team, has not agreed with the objectives, there will be no commitment to achieving them.

Realistic

If the objectives are not realistic, the project team will soon realize that and lose any commitment to the project.

Timed

If there is no pressure to complete the project, it will never get completed.

Note: some people use a different set of words for the SMART acronym (e.g. Specific, Measurable, Assignable or Achievable, Realistic and Time-related). It doesn't matter which words you use, as long as they achieve a similar effect.

Hot tip

If you haven't already done so, define your project objectives now and make sure they are SMART.

Step 2: Develop the Plan

Having defined your project objectives, the next step is to plan how you will achieve them (how you will get there), by developing the project plan.

Before we start developing the plan, we need to look at some of the basic elements that make up a project plan. These are Tasks, Deliverables, Milestones and Resources:

Tasks

Tasks are the basic building blocks of the project. They represent the work that has to be carried out in order to complete the project. They will need to be carried out in some sort of timed sequence, and they will also be interdependent with one or more other tasks.

Deliverables

Deliverables (sometimes referred to as the products of a project) are the things that will be produced or delivered by the project along the way. Typically, they consist of progress or management reports, specifications of requirements, design documents and agreements, as well as the final result of the project (whatever that may be).

Milestones

Milestones are the points during the project where you can accurately measure the progress. They will typically be major events, such as an agreement of requirements, approval of funding or final acceptance.

Resources

Resources are the people and other things (material and finance) you will use on the project in order to carry out the tasks, produce the deliverables, and meet the milestones.

To put these into the context of the project plan, the plan will set out the *Tasks* needed to produce the *Deliverables* and complete the project. It will also set out the *Resources* you will need to carry out the tasks, and the *Milestones* you will use to measure your progress. The time line, or schedule, will set out when these things should happen.

The following topics in this chapter will look at Tasks, Deliverables, Milestones and Resources in more detail.

Hot tip

Deliverables provide the best way of measuring project progress.

Tasks and Deliverables

Any project consists of a number of tasks that need to be completed. Depending on the project, it may consist of very few tasks or it may involve many tasks. Some of these tasks will be relatively short, while others will take much longer to complete. Some will be critical to the success of the project, while others may be less important.

Having defined or clarified the objectives, the first step in producing your project plan is to begin listing the key tasks, these are the important ones, the ones that are critical to the success of the project. These will typically be related to a key deliverable. For example, if you were building a house, there would be a "design" task, which would have the "house plans" as its deliverable.

If, for example, your project was a feasibility study, the key tasks and deliverables could be something like this:

Key Tasks	Deliverables
Agree the Objectives	Objectives
Plan the Study	Study Plan
Information Gathering	Interview Notes
Produce Draft Requirements	Draft Requirements
Hold Feedback Sessions	Final Requirements
Develop Recommendations	Recommendations
Perform Risk Analysis	Risk Log
Produce Implementation Plan	Implementation Plan
Report to Management	Final Report

While you may well have many other tasks to carry out during your project, and may have other deliverables you need to produce, these should represent the major ones.

If you are not sure whether a task is a key task or not, play safe and include it. It is easy to remove something later, if it is not required, but missing something important at the start could be fatal to a project.

Milestones

Project milestones are the events that mark the completion of a major task, or group of tasks, in a project.

Typical milestones would be the decision to proceed, selection of a supplier, acceptance of a major piece of work and, of course, completion of the project. Milestones often mark the acceptance of a key deliverable.

A milestone normally has a zero duration. In other words, it marks a single point in time when something happens.

Once you have identified the key tasks, and their deliverables, in your project, you need to identify the major milestones. For a short project (such as a feasibility study), there may only be one milestone: completion of the study.

In the illustration above, the final task is a milestone, it has a zero duration and is indicated by a black diamond, with the date on the right-hand side of the Gantt chart.

It is also possible to give a milestone a duration and still mark it as a milestone. This is covered in the next chapter.

For a longer project, there may be more milestones, typically between three and eight. So once you have identified all your key tasks, take another look at your project and identify what you think your project milestones are.

In the next chapter, we will look at how to enter and link tasks and milestones.

Step 3: Carry it Out

If you've been through Step 1 (Define the Objectives) and Step 2 (Develop the Plan), then you know where you're going (the Objectives) and you know how you are going to get there (the Plan). Now you can start carrying out the project by allocating the tasks to the resources who will be doing them.

Resources

The key resources on most projects are the people who will be doing the work (including the project manager). In Project, resources are entered in the Resource Sheet.

1. Click on the Resource tab and the down arrow beside Team Planner to open the list of built in views, as illustrated on the right

2. Select resource sheet (fourth item on list) and the Resource sheet view will open, as illustrated below:

Resource Name ▼	Type ▼	Material ▼	Initials ▼	Group ▼	Max. ▼	Std. Rate ▼
Prudence Project	Work		PP	PM	100%	$0.00/hr
Joe Soap	Work		JS	Marketing	100%	$0.00/hr
Mary Dee	Work		MD	Finance	100%	$0.00/hr
Wendy Page	Work		WP	IT	100%	$0.00/hr
Bill Buggs	Work		BB	Exec	100%	$0.00/hr

3. Type in the names, initials and groups for all the people who will be working on your project

4. If you have a resource requirement, but don't yet know who it will be, just enter the role (e.g. Accountant) in the resource name column (you can change it later)

5. You can enter information in the other columns (not all illustrated above), if you have it, or leave the default values in for the time being

The resources defined above are all Work (this is the default for human resources or people). You can also define Material and Cost resources. These resource types are all covered in more detail in chapter 7 (Resources).

Saving Your Project

The chances are that, sooner or later, everyone who works with a computer will lose a large amount of work through a power cut, or some other problem outside their of control. Project 2010 is no exception to this, so save your work regularly.

By saving your work regularly, you will also be able to try things out and always get back to where you were.

1 To save your file (replacing the previous version), click the Save button on the Quick Access Toolbar or use the keyboard short cut: Ctrl+S

2 If you want to preserve the previous version of the project, select the File tab and then select Save As from the drop down file list to open the Save As dialog box, as illustrated below

3 Select the directory where you want to save the file, give it a new file name and click Save

4 If you want to save the project file so that it can be opened in an earlier version of Project, click on the down arrow beside "Save as type" and select the appropriate version (Project 2007 or Project 2000 to 2003)

Step 4: Hand it Over

Once the project is completed, the project manager's role is finished. However, some project managers have problems with this final step.

Letting Go

You have to let go and let the people who will be responsible for the ongoing operation take over managing the process. They won't like it, or feel comfortable, if the project manager is looking over their shoulders the whole time, so let them get on with it. You should have planned any required training for them and, once they are up to speed, they will be fine.

Provide Support

But you cannot just drop a new process on the people who have to make it work and run! They will almost certainly have some problems adapting to new ways of doing things. What you must do is be available if they need you. This means scheduling some of your time to support the people carrying out the new process. This should only be for an initial, short, critical period (usually in the region of a month).

Finish the Paperwork

The hand over time is a great opportunity to finish off any outstanding paperwork or documentation. Tidy up the project files and back everything up.

Project Review

The last scheduled task on the project should be to arrange and hold a post-implementation review. This is the time when you can go back to the original objectives and see if they have been achieved or not. Was there anything that happened during the project that could not be dealt with or included in the project? If there was, should another project be initiated to deal with it?

As part of this review, the methods and tools used on the project should also be examined, and anything learned should be noted for the benefit of future projects.

Thank the Team

Last, but not least, don't forget to thank everyone who helped you with the project, they will appreciate it. One of the nicest ways of thanking the project team is to take them out for a project team celebration meal.

Hot tip

Always invite your project sponsor and, with any luck, they will pick up the bill.

Summary

- Take a structured, 4-Step approach to project management: first define the objectives; second, develop the plan; then you can carry it out; and, finally, hand it over when it is completed

- When defining your objectives it is good to check if they are SMART: that means Strategic, Measurable, Agreed, Realistic and Timed

- Begin to develop your project plan by identifying the Tasks to be carried out, Deliverables that will be produced, the project Milestones that you will use to measure progress and the Resources you will need to do the work

- Try to identify all the critical, key (or important) tasks that need to be done, together with their associated deliverables, at the outset

- Identify how many project milestones you will need and where they should go. Milestones are entered just like tasks, but with a zero duration

- In order to carry out the project, you will need to define the human (people) and other resources you will need on your project. Details of these are entered in Resource Sheet view. If you don't know who they will be yet, use a dummy name for the time being

- Remember to save your project file regularly when you are making changes to it, and to save it back into an earlier format if you need to send it to someone with an earlier version of Project

- Handing the project over can sometimes be difficult but it has to be done. It is a useful opportunity to tidy things up and make sure everything is in place for on-going support before handing it over

- Once everything has been handed over, it is then time to carry out a review of how well the project went

- Finally, don't forget to thank the people who helped you on the project, including your project sponsor

4 Working with Tasks

Tasks represent the basic building blocks of a project, while milestones are the reference points used to measure progress. This chapter will show the uses of tasks and milestones in creating the basic project plan.

46 Creating a Task

48 Task Duration

49 Adding Tasks

50 Task Dependencies

51 Linking Tasks

52 Unlinking Tasks

53 Changing Dependencies

54 Moving a Task

55 Deleting a Task

56 Task Form

57 Project Milestones

58 Recurring Tasks

59 Work Effort v Duration

60 Summary

Creating a Task

Tasks represent the basic building blocks of the project plan. They represent the pieces of work that will have to be done in order to carry out the project. Tasks can be entered in any view that includes a Task Name field, but the (default) Gantt chart view is the easiest one to use in the build up of the task list.

1 Open a project file, or to create a new one, select the Task tab and Gantt chart view (if you are not already in it)

Auto Schedule

In Project 2010, you can insert tasks using auto scheduling or manual scheduling. For auto scheduling:

2 Click on Mode (as illustrated above) and select Auto Schedule

3 Click in the first Task Name field, type in the task name (e.g. Agree Project Objectives) and then press Enter

Hot tip

The collapsed view on the right was produced using the Show/Hide Ribbon.

A Task ID (identity) of 1 is assigned to the task (on the left-hand side above) and the default duration of 1 day is allocated. The question mark after the duration indicates that it is the default (estimated) duration. The task is scheduled to start on today's date (or the start date of the project, if you have changed it) and a 1 day bar is shown on the Gantt chart to the right.

Manual Schedule

If manual scheduling mode is selected in place of auto scheduling (at step 2 opposite) and the task name is entered (as in step 3 opposite), the following is the result:

As can be seen, the task ID of 1 is allocated and the task name is inserted, but no duration or start date is assumed. In manual schedule mode you would need to enter these manually. This mode is useful if you have identified the tasks but have not yet estimated the durations, or when they will be scheduled.

Wrap Text

If the task name you type in is longer than the width of the column, the text will wrap to the next line, as in the following illustration:

If you do not want the text to wrap, you can make the column wider by dragging the edge of the column header to the right, as illustrated.

Wrap text is the default setting, but it can be changed, if required, by de-selecting the wrap text function (as illustrated right) on the Format tab. Now any extra text will be hidden from view unless the Task Name column width is adjusted, as above.

Hot tip

You can also select and de-select wrap text by right clicking on the task name header.

47

Task Duration

When auto-scheduling is selected, new tasks are created with an estimated duration of one day. The estimated duration is indicated by the question mark after the 1 day. Once you enter a duration, the question mark will be removed. The duration can be changed by using the spin controls or by typing directly into the field.

 Click on the duration field and use the spin controls (the up and down arrows that appear when the field is selected) to increase or reduce it

	❶	Task Name	▾	Duration ▾	Start ▾		'11 W T F S S M T W T	Jul 04, '11
1		Agree Project Objectives		2 days ⬍	Fri 07/01/11			

Note, in the illustration above, that the bar on the Gantt chart is showing the duration as two working days (Saturday and Sunday being non-working days by default).

You can also click on the Duration field and type in a number. It will default to the existing time type (days in this example).

 To change the duration time type, you need to enter the number followed by m (minutes), h (hours), d (days), w (weeks) or mo (months)

	❶	Task Name	▾	Duration ▾	Start ▾		'11 W T F S S M T W T F S S	Jul 04, '11
1		Agree Project Objectives		24 hrs ⬍	Fri 07/01/11			

Note, in the illustration above, that 24 hours is scheduled to take three working days. The scheduling default is 8 hours working time per day, so 24 hours is three working days.

 If you need to enter an elapsed time (rather than working time) duration, you can do so by typing an "e" in front of the time type, so "24eh" will be interpreted and scheduled as illustrated below:

	❶	Task Name	▾	Duration ▾	Start ▾	Jun 27, '11 M T W T F S
1		Agree Project Objectives		24 ehrs ⬍	Fri 07/01/11	

Adding Tasks

Additional tasks can be added to a project at any time. The tasks can be added after existing tasks, or inserted in between or in front of existing tasks. We will look at doing both.

1 To add new tasks to the end, click on the first blank Task Name field and type in your new task name, press the tab key, type in the duration and then press Enter

2 To insert a new task into an existing task list, click on the task name that you wish to insert the new task in front of, then click New Task on the Task ribbon

Hot tip

You can also use the keyboard Insert key as a short-cut for inserting a new task.

3 Type in the new task name, tab to the duration field and enter the duration

The new task is inserted in the required position, as illustrated above. Continue adding tasks as above to build up your task list.

Task Dependencies

Tasks do not exist in isolation, most will be dependant on one or more other tasks, and they will have one or more other tasks dependant on them. The only exceptions are the first and last task in the project.

In the following illustration, task 2 requires something from and is therefore dependant on task 1 being completed before it can begin. In a similar way, task 3 is dependant on task 2.

In Project 2010, you create these dependencies by linking the appropriate tasks. Linking tasks allows you to specify the circumstances where the start or finish of a task is dependant on the start or finish of another task or set of tasks.

Finish-to-start

The most common type of dependency or link is the finish-to-start dependency (as illustrated above), where the finish of task 1 allows task 2 to start. Typically, this is where task 2 needs something that is produced in task 1.

On the Gantt chart, the link is shown as illustrated on the right.

There are three other types of links:

Start-to-start

This is where task 2 can start at the same time as task 1 and can take place at the same time. It is shown on the Gantt chart as illustrated right.

Finish-to-finish

This is used where task 2 has to finish at the same time as task 1 and is shown as illustrated right.

Start-to-finish

In this case, when task 1 starts task 2 must finish and is shown as illustrated on the right.

These three (and particularly the last one) are likely to be the exception rather than the rule.

Beware

It is best to avoid the start-to-finish link, if possible, as it can cause some problems.

50

Linking Tasks

Task dependencies are created by linking tasks. The default dependency is the finish-to-start dependency, and this will normally be the way you will want to link most of the tasks in your project. The quickest approach is to link all the tasks in this way to start with and then make any required changes.

1 In Gantt chart view, click on the Task Name column header to select all your tasks

	🛈	Task Name	Duration	Start	Jun 27, '11		Jul 04, '11	
					M T W T F S S	M T W T F S S		
1		Agree Project Objectives	1 day	Fri 07/01/11				
2		Identify Stakeholders	1 day	Fri 07/01/11				
3		Select Project Team	2 days	Fri 07/01/11				
4		Produce Outline Plan	1 day	Fri 07/01/11				
5		Identify Business Case	2 days	Fri 07/01/11				
6		Risk Analysis	1 day	Fri 07/01/11				

Hot tip

You can also select several tasks by dragging your cursor across the task names or task IDs.

2 Click the Link tasks function (as illustrated on the right) on the Task ribbon

	🛈	Task Name	Duration	Start	Jun 27, '11	Jul 04, '11	Jul 11, '11
					M T W T F S S	M T W T F S S	M T W T F
1		Agree Project Objectives	1 day	Fri 07/01/11			
2		Identify Stakeholders	1 day	Mon 07/04/11			
3		Select Project Team	2 days	Tue 07/05/11			
4		Produce Outline Plan	1 day	Thu 07/07/11			
5		Identify Business Case	2 days	Fri 07/08/11			
6		Risk Analysis	1 day	Tue 07/12/11			

The tasks are now all linked in a finish-to-start dependency. The start dates are adjusted so that each task starts when its predecessor finishes.

You can also link tasks by holding down the Ctrl key, clicking the individual task names, and then clicking the Link tasks button.

Links are always created in the direction in which you select the tasks. Selecting task 2 and then task 1 will result in a link from task 2 to task 1. Task 1 will then be dependent on task 2.

3 If you are happy with the way your tasks are linked, save your project file before you start changing anything else. Try to get into the habit of saving your project file each time you make a change

Unlinking Tasks

If you have just completed the previous topic, you will have linked all the tasks in the project in a finish-to-start dependency. You may now need to unlink some of them.

1 Select the two tasks you wish to unlink (hold down the Ctrl key and click on the two task names)

2 Click the Unlink tasks function (as illustrated right) on the Task ribbon and the link is removed, as illustrated below

3 An alternative way of accessing the link between tasks is to double-click on the link line between the two tasks you wish to unlink on the Gantt chart. This will open the Task Dependency dialog box

4 Click Delete and the link is removed

You can also unlink several tasks at the same time by selecting them all and then clicking the Unlink button.

Changing Dependencies

Although the majority of tasks in a project will normally be in a finish-to-start dependency, you will sometimes need to change the dependency to one of the other types.

1 In Gantt chart view, double-click on the link line between the two tasks where you wish to change the dependency. This will bring up the Task Dependency dialog box

2 Click on the down arrow to the right of Type to bring up the drop-down list of options (as illustrated above)

3 Select the required option and click OK

In the following illustration, Start-to-Start (SS) was selected at Step 3 above and the two tasks have now been rescheduled to start on the same day:

The four types of dependency were defined on page 50 (Task Dependencies). Selecting Finish-to-Finish (FF) or Start-to-Finish (SF) will link the tasks as illustrated on that page.

To change the dependency back to the way it was originally, repeat steps one and two above and select Finish-to-Start (FS) from the drop down list.

Selecting (None) on the drop-down list of options removes the dependency and is, therefore, another way of unlinking tasks.

Moving a Task

If you wish to move a task to a new position in the task list, the easiest way is to use drag-and-drop. Select the ID of the task (or tasks) that you want to move and drag it to its new position.

1 Click once on the Task ID of the task you want to move to select the whole task and then release the mouse button

2 Now click on the task ID again, but this time do not release the mouse button and drag the task up or down the task list as required. Notice the insertion point marker (see shaded line above) as you drag

3 When you get to the desired new location, release the mouse button

The task is moved to its new location (as illustrated above) and the links have been retained. You may wish to change them if they are no longer appropriate.

4 To re-link the task in its new position, you could remove the existing links and replace them with links from tasks 4 and 5 to task 6, which will reschedule the moved task (as illustrated below)

Deleting a Task

If you need to delete a task from a task list, simply select it and delete it as follows:

1 Select the task to be deleted by clicking on its Task ID, which selects the whole task

	ⓘ	Task Name	Duration	Start	Jun 27, '11	Jul 04, '11	Jul 11, '11
					M T W T F S S	M T W T F S S	M T W T
1		Agree Project Objectives	1 day	Fri 07/01/11			
2		Identify Stakeholders	1 day	Mon 07/04/11			
3		Select Project Team	2 days	Tue 07/05/11			
4		Identify Business Case	2 days	Thu 07/07/11			
5		Risk Analysis	1 day	Thu 07/07/11			
6		Produce Outline Plan	1 day	Mon 07/11/11			

2 Then press the keyboard Delete key and the task is removed from the project

	ⓘ	Task Name	Duration	Start	Jun 27, '11	Jul 04, '11	Jul 11, '11
					M T W T F S S	M T W T F S S	M T W T
1		Agree Project Objectives	1 day	Fri 07/01/11			
2		Select Project Team	2 days	Fri 07/01/11			
3		Identify Business Case	2 days	Tue 07/05/11			
4		Risk Analysis	1 day	Tue 07/05/11			
5		Produce Outline Plan	1 day	Thu 07/07/11			

3 If you delete the wrong task (or tasks) in error, you can reverse your previous actions using the Undo function (as illustrated right) on the quick access toolbar

4 You can also delete individual fields or whole tasks by selecting the Task name and pressing the Delete key. This will bring up a smart tag asking you to confirm what you want to delete (see below)

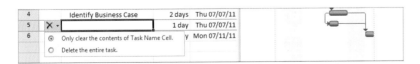

4		Identify Business Case	2 days	Thu 07/07/11	
5	✕ ▾			1 day	Thu 07/07/11
6	◉	Only clear the contents of Task Name Cell.		y	Mon 07/11/11
	○	Delete the entire task.			

5 Click on "Only clear the contents of the selected cell" to clear that field, or "Delete the entire task" and the whole task will be deleted

As with step three, if you make a mistake you can always use the Undo function on the quick access toolbar.

Task Form

Task Form view (which displays the task details) is one of the built-in views available in Project. It is used to enter, view and edit details of individual tasks.

1 Click on the arrow next to Gantt chart view on the Task ribbon to display the built in views (as illustrated on the right) and select Task Form to display this view

Although this view is useful to work on task details, there is another option:

2 Click the View tab to display the View ribbon (as illustrated below)

3 Select the Details option in the Split screen group and the Task Form is displayed in the lower half of the screen (as illustrated below)

4 You can now view, enter and edit task details directly in the lower pane, and any changes made in either pane will be reflected in the other

5 The split bar (shown in black in the illustration above) can be moved up or down as required and double-clicking on it will hide the Task Form and return to the basic Gantt chart view

Project Milestones

Project milestones represent the significant events that mark the progress of a project. Any task can be made into a milestone by setting the duration to zero. You can also insert a milestone using the Task ribbon:

1 Select the task you want to insert a milestone in front of, and then click the insert milestone function on the Task ribbon

2 Type in the milestone name and link any tasks the milestone is dependant on

3 To add a duration to the milestone, click in the Duration field and enter a duration, then click the Information function (to the right of Insert Milestone) on the Task ribbon to open the task dialog box

Hot tip

You can also double-click the Task Name to open the Task Information dialog box

4 Select the Advanced tab, check Mark Task as Milestone (bottom left) and click OK. The task will be shown as a milestone with a duration (as illustrated below)

Recurring Tasks

Any task that is regularly repeated in a project is called a recurring task. It could be a project team meeting, a meeting with your project sponsor or the production of a monthly report.

The procedure for setting up a recurring task is different from creating a normal task, and you cannot convert a normal task into a recurring task.

1 To insert a recurring task, click the down arrow beneath the Insert task function on the Task ribbon, select Recurring task and the Recurring Task Information dialog box will open (as illustrated below)

2 Enter the task name, duration, recurrence and range information (as in the above example) and click OK

The recurring task is inserted into the task list. The "+" next to the task name indicates that it consists of a number of subtasks (one for each meeting in this case). Clicking on the "+" will display the individual meeting sub-tasks. Double-clicking on the task name will bring up the Recurring Task Information dialog box again, to allow any further editing.

Work Effort v Duration

One of the principal reasons for breaking a project down into tasks is that it is far easier to plan, allocate and control smaller packets of work. This topic is concerned with the process of estimating how much work a task will require (the work effort) and how long it will take to complete that work (the duration). Be warned, the two are very rarely the same.

Work Effort

When it comes to estimating how much work will be involved in a task, you can base it on one (or a combination) of four options:

- Experience: if you have done a similar task before, you can base it on how much work effort that task required

- Advice: if you know someone who has done something similar, you can ask them how much work it involved

- Guidelines: your organization or industry may have guidelines for estimating that you can use

- Guess: if none of the other options are available to you, then your guess is probably as good as anyone else's

So that gives you an initial estimate of how much work is involved in the task, but how long will it actually take the person who is going to do it?

Duration

Microsoft Project basically treats work effort and duration in a fairly simplistic way. If you double the resources on a task, it will halve the duration. It does not usually work like that in real life.

Duration will be dependant on the amount of time the person carrying out the task has available, and what other work they have to do at the same time. If they are allocated to your project 100% of the time there will be fewer problems, but that is rarely the case.

The most effective way is to ask the person who will be doing it how long it will take them. But, in the early stages of planning a project, you won't always know who will be doing the work. In the absence of anything else, a factor of 50% would be sensible, so, if it looks like about 4 days work effort, you should set the duration to 6 days, assuming that one person will do it.

Summary

- Tasks are the basic building blocks of a project plan and they are best entered in Gantt chart view

- Auto-schedule allows Project to schedule the start date of a task, while manual schedule allows you to enter the start date

- If the task name is too large for the column, Project will wrap the text to the next line unless you over-ride it

- Task duration can be defined in minutes, hours, days, weeks or even months and it can be typed in or set using the spinner controls

- Tasks can be added to the end of a task list or they can be inserted using the New Task function (or the Insert key); they will be inserted in front of the selected task

- There are four types of task dependency: finish-to-start is the most common dependency, but tasks can also be linked in finish-to-finish, start-to-start or start-to-finish

- Tasks are linked to form dependencies using the link task button and can also be unlinked using the unlink task button

- Task dependencies can be changed or deleted by double-clicking on the link line between the tasks

- Tasks can be moved up or down the task list by selecting the task and dragging it up or down to its new place. You may also need to change the dependency links after this move

- Tasks can be deleted using the Delete key and smart tag

- The undo button can reverse any mistakes you may make

- The task form can be applied to the Gantt chart to give more detail and control over a task

- Project milestones are created as tasks with zero duration or they can be set through the task information dialog box

- Recurring tasks need to be set up using Insert Recurring Task from the Task ribbon

- When estimating task duration, it is important to remember that the duration is rarely the same as the work effort

Don't forget

The person most likely to know how long a task will take is the person who will be doing it.

5 Adding Structure

In this chapter, we start to add some structure to the project by developing summary tasks and subtasks and using outlining.

62 Project Structure

63 Summary Tasks

64 Project Stages

66 Changing the Timescale

67 Outline Numbering

68 Subtasks

70 Summary

Project Structure

A simple project, such as carrying out a feasibility study, might consist of no more than 10 or 12 tasks. A medium-sized project, such as introducing a new business venture or planning and organizing an exhibition, could run into over one hundred individual tasks. While a very large project, such as building a new airport, could run into many thousands of tasks.

Work Breakdown Structure

If you try to identify and plan every single task in your project right from the start, you will almost certainly be doomed to failure. In the early stages of a project there are just too many uncertainties and unknown factors, which will only become known as the project progresses. To cope with this, a project needs to be broken down into manageable chunks, one level at a time. This is known as the Work Breakdown Structure (WBS).

Work Breakdown Structure

First we break the project down into its main stages

Project

Stage 1   Stage 2

Then we break each stage down into its tasks

Task 1.1   Task 1.2   Task 2.1

1   First break your project down into discrete chunks, with their own major deliverables, these are usually referred to as Stages (but they may also be called Phases)

2   Then, in turn, break each Stage into the Tasks that will be needed to carry it out

3   Finally, each Task may also need to be broken down into one (or more) level of Subtasks (not shown in the diagram above), depending on the size of the project and the size of the task

Summary Tasks

In Microsoft Project, structure is implemented through Subtasks and Summary Tasks. Any task that has a subtask is itself a summary task. Therefore, a task can be a subtask of another task and a summary task itself. Project Stages are summary tasks.

A summary task is created in similar way to any other task but its subtasks are indented.

1 Select the tasks you want to insert a summary task for and then click on Insert Summary Task on the Task ribbon

Don't forget

You can select multiple tasks by holding down the Ctrl key and clicking on each task, or by dragging your cursor down the Task IDs.

The new summary task is inserted and the selected tasks have been made its sub-tasks, as illustrated below:

2 Type in the name for the summary task and press Enter, the job is done

Note that individual tasks can also be promoted to summary tasks or demoted to sub-tasks by selecting the task and using the Indent and Outdent functions on the Task ribbon (as illustrated on the right)

Project Stages

Conventionally, in project management methodology, the first-level summary tasks are referred to as project stages.

Project management methodology initially grew out of the construction industry, and it still retains some of that industry's terminology. In later years, it has also been influenced by the information technology industry, which, interestingly, has a lot of similarities.

Using that influence, we can now build a little further on our 4-step approach by expanding our second step (plan how we will get there) into two separate stages. The first is to determine what the detailed business needs are and the second is to define what we will need to do to achieve those needs.

If this sounds a bit like "overkill", keep an open mind for the time being. Hopefully, as we develop the process further, you will begin to see why this is a useful approach. These five project stages are conventionally referred to as:

Initiation
To define the project objectives and the team structure, produce the initial (outline) project plan and get the project started.

Strategy
To determine what the detailed business needs are and what the potential payback will be when we achieve them.

Analysis
To define what will need to be done in order to meet the business needs.

Design and Build
Carrying out the project by doing the detailed design of how it will be done and then doing it (i.e. build it, buy it, etc.).

Implementation
To install and hand over the new process and close the project.

The chief benefit of this approach is that the major expense or effort usually occurs in the Design and Build stage. At each of the preceding stages, the potential investment and benefits can be reappraised to ensure that it will still be viable. If not, the project can be wound up with minimal cost to the business.

Hot tip

There is nothing sacred about these five stages or their names. They are just a suggested starting point, and they should be adapted to suit your own project.

Adding Project Stages

Having decided on the number of stages, you can initially add them to the project with a dummy task under each. These can be replaced later, when you have identified the real tasks.

1 If you have not already created the first project stage in the Summary Task topic (page 63), do it now

2 Then select the Task where you want to insert your next stage and click the Insert Summary Task function in the Task ribbon

In the example above, there were no existing tasks where the new stage was inserted so Project has inserted a dummy task as well. Note that the new stage has been inserted at the same level as the preceding task, so it will need to be outdented.

3 Type in the stage name, dummy task name, dummy task duration and outdent the stage, if required, using outdent, as illustrated right

4 Link the last task in the first stage to the first task in the second stage

Continue inserting stages (and dummy tasks, with durations where required) and linking them as above. Ideally, all the tasks in the project should be linked and, on completion, your project should look something like the first illustration on the following page (overleaf).

Changing the Timescale

Once you begin to link all the tasks in a project, they will quickly vanish off the timescale in the right-hand pane and you won't be able to see the whole project. This is easily remedied.

1 Select the View tab and click on Entire Project on the View ribbon to bring the whole project into view

2 Click on the Task Name header to select all tasks, click Outline on the View ribbon and select Outline Level 1 from the drop-down list (as illustrated right), to display the top-level view of your project, with just the stages showing (as illustrated below)

You can use Outline>All Subtasks from the View ribbon to bring all the tasks back into view, and use Zoom>Zoom In, Out and Custom from the View ribbon to get more or less details into view. Finally, select Timescale>Days from the View ribbon to get back to a days within weeks view (as illustrated below):

Outline Numbering

For a small project with very few tasks, the Task ID number is probably a good enough way of numbering your tasks. But, for larger projects, a more structured way of numbering, that reflects the Work Breakdown Structure (WBS), will be needed. Outline numbering gives you a simple way of achieving this.

1 Select the Format tab and click Outline Numbering on the Format ribbon

Your stages and tasks will now be numbered in a structured format. Stages being numbered 1, 2, 3 etc. and tasks being numbered 1.1, 1.2, 1.3 etc. (as illustrated below).

If an additional level of subtasks is inserted below task 1.3, they will be numbered 1.3.1, 1.3.2 and so on.

One result of the addition of the numbers to the task name is that some of the task names may get truncated. You could resolve this by selecting Wrap Text from the Format ribbon, or by increasing the size of the field by dragging the edge of the Task Name header (as illustrated on page 47).

Subtasks

Creating additional layers of subtasks is a similar process to creating summary tasks, but, instead of inserting a summary task and outdenting it, we insert the subtasks and indent them. This then turns the task above them into a summary task

1 Select the task in front of which you wish to insert the subtasks and then click Insert Task on the Task ribbon once for each new subtask to be inserted:

2 Type in the new subtask names and their durations (in the example below, Interview Managers and Interview Staff, both with 2 days duration)

Notice that they have been treated as tasks at the same level as the task above them and that they have not been linked or indented:

3 Select the two tasks by Ctrl+clicking on them and clicking Indent on the Task ribbon

The two subtasks have now been numbered 2.1.1 and 2.1.2 and their summary task 2.1 is now in bold (as illustrated below).

	❶	Task Name	Duration	Start	Jul 18, '11	Jul 25, '11	Aug 01, '11
8		1.7 Project Approval	5 days	Tue 07/12/11	◆ 07/18		
9		2 Strategy Stage	19 days	Tue 07/19/11			
10		2.1 Interviews	2 days	Tue 07/19/11			
11		2.1.1 Interview Managers	2 days	Tue 07/19/11			
12		2.1.2 Interview Staff	2 days	Tue 07/19/11			
13		2.2 Draft Requirements	2 days	Thu 07/21/11			
14		2.3 Feedback Sessions	1 day	Mon 07/25/11			

As can be seen from the above illustration, the tasks have not yet been linked, so we need to complete that step:

4 Select the two tasks and click the Link function on the Task ribbon to link the two tasks

	❶	Task Name	Duration	Start	Jul 18, '11	Jul 25, '11	Aug 01, '11
9		2 Strategy Stage	21 days	Tue 07/19/11			
10		2.1 Interviews	4 days	Tue 07/19/11			
11		2.1.1 Interview Managers	2 days	Tue 07/19/11			
12		2.1.2 Interview Staff	2 days	Thu 07/21/11			
13		2.2 Draft Requirements	2 days	Mon 07/25/11			
14		2.3 Feedback Sessions	1 day	Wed 07/27/11			
15		2.4 Finalize Requirements	2 days	Thu 07/28/11			
16		2.5 Review Risks	1 day	Mon 08/01/11			
17		2.6 Forward Plan	2 days	Tue 08/02/11			
18		2.7 Report to Management	1 day	Thu 08/04/11			
19		2.8 Contingency	8 days	Fri 08/05/11			

As can be seen from the illustration above, the subtasks are now linked but the summary task (2.1 Interviews) has the links from and to the preceding and succeeding tasks. Ideally, these links should be changed to go to and from the subtasks to maintain task dependencies at the lowest level, as illustrated below:

	❶	Task Name	Duration	Start	Jul 18, '11	Jul 25, '11	Aug 01, '11
8		1.7 Project Approval	5 days	Tue 07/12/11	◆ 07/18		
9		2 Strategy Stage	21 days	Tue 07/19/11			
10		2.1 Interviews	4 days	Tue 07/19/11			
11		2.1.1 Interview Managers	2 days	Tue 07/19/11			
12		2.1.2 Interview Staff	2 days	Thu 07/21/11			
13		2.2 Draft Requirements	2 days	Mon 07/25/11			

Visual Change Highlights

The other feature to note in the top two screen shots above is that, as we make changes to the schedule, the changes are highlighted in light blue in the table on the left hand side.

In the third screen shot, we have changed the dependency links, but this has not impacted the schedule so nothing is highlighted.

Hot tip

When building up a stage schedule, it is a good idea to include some contingency for the (as yet) unknown.

Summary

- The way the tasks in a project are structured is referred to as the Work Breakdown Structure (WBS). The best approach is to break the project down one stage and one level at a time, as more information becomes known

- A summary task is any task that has subtasks beneath it, and, with multiple levels, a task can be both a subtask and a summary task

- Outdenting is the process in Project that promotes a task to a summary task, while Indenting is the process that demotes a task to a subtask

- The first-level tasks in a structure are normally called the project stages and are always summary tasks. There will normally be between three and eight stages in a project and a standard set of five (Initiation, Strategy, Analysis, Design & Build, and Implementation) are suggested as a starting point

- Stages are created in a project by inserting them as summary tasks and indenting the tasks beneath them to make them subtasks of the stage

- As you start to build up your project structure, you can zoom in and out to change the timescale and show different outline levels. This facility lets you move between the big picture and the detail

- Although you can create a custom WBS in Project, the built in outline numbering function can provide a simple, numeric reference, which reflects the WBS at each level

- Subtasks are created by inserting new tasks below an existing task and then indenting them

- As you start to build up your project plan, it is a good idea to include some contingency at the end of each stage to reflect the unknown things that will only be discovered later in the project

- Visual change highlights reflect any change by highlighting all durations and dates that have changed as a result of the last change made

6 More About Tasks

This chapter goes into Tasks in a little more detail. It introduces lag time and lead time, task notes, setting deadline dates, critical path and moving linked tasks.

72 Lag Time and Lead Time

74 Task Inspector

75 Task Notes

76 Deadline Dates

77 Moving Around

78 Critical Path

79 Critical Tasks

80 Splitting Tasks

81 Moving Linked Tasks

82 Summary

Lag Time and Lead Time

Up to now we have been linking tasks, mainly in a finish-to-start dependency, with the next task starting immediately after the preceding task finishes. However, there are times when you will want the tasks to have a gap or overlap between them, and we do this by using lag time and lead time.

Lag Time

Lag time is when there is a gap (or lag) between the finish of one task and the start of the next task. This is input using the Lag time field on the Task Dependency dialog box. In the following example, we want to introduce a 2 day lag between the end of Task 1.1 Agree Project Objectives and the start of Task 1.2 Identify Stakeholders.

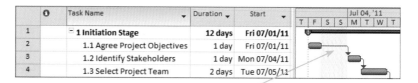

1 Double-click on the line connecting the two tasks where you want to add lag time to open the Task Dependency dialog box

2 Change the Lag time using the spinner controls, or by typing in the required duration, and click OK

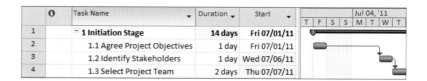

The dependent task will be rescheduled and the link line will be extended to the length of the lag time. Any other tasks linked to the dependant task will also be rescheduled by Project.

Lead Time

Lead time is where there is an overlap, with the next task starting before the previous task has finished. This is also input using the Lag time field, but using a negative number to represent lead time. In the following example, we want to introduce a 1 day lead time between Task 1.3 Select Project Team and Task 1.4 Identify Business Case.

	ⓘ	Task Name	Duration	Start		Jul 04, '11	Jul 11, '11
						T F S S M T W T F S	S M T W
1		⊟ **1 Initiation Stage**	**14 days**	**Fri 07/01/11**			
2		1.1 Agree Project Objectives	1 day	Fri 07/01/11			
3		1.2 Identify Stakeholders	1 day	Wed 07/06/11			
4		1.3 Select Project Team	2 days	Thu 07/07/11			
5		1.4 Identify Business Case	2 days	Mon 07/11/11			
6		1.5 Risk Analysis	1 day	Mon 07/11/11			
7		1.6 Produce Outline Plan	1 day	Wed 07/13/11			
8		1.7 Project Approval	5 days	Thu 07/14/11			

1 Double-click on the connecting line between the two tasks where you want to include lead time to open the Task Dependency dialog box

2 Change the Lag time using the down spinner control, or type a negative number to represent the lead time duration, and click OK

	ⓘ	Task Name	Duration	Start		Jul 04, '11	Jul 11, '11
						T F S S M T W T F S	S M T W
1		⊟ **1 Initiation Stage**	**13 days**	**Fri 07/01/11**			
2		1.1 Agree Project Objectives	1 day	Fri 07/01/11			
3		1.2 Identify Stakeholders	1 day	Wed 07/06/11			
4		1.3 Select Project Team	2 days	Thu 07/07/11			
5		1.4 Identify Business Case	2 days	Fri 07/08/11			
6		1.5 Risk Analysis	1 day	Fri 07/08/11			
7		1.6 Produce Outline Plan	1 day	Tue 07/12/11			

The dependent task has been brought forward and now starts one day before the preceding task finishes. In the above example, the task following the dependant task has also been brought forward to overlap by one day, due to its start-to-start dependency.

Task Inspector

Task inspect allows you to view the constraints and dependencies that impact a task's start date. They can help you to establish the factor or factors that may be delaying a task, such as task dependency, calendar constraints, schedule date, holidays or vacation.

 In Gantt chart view, click Inspect on the Tasks ribbon to open the task inspector panel to the left of the task sheet

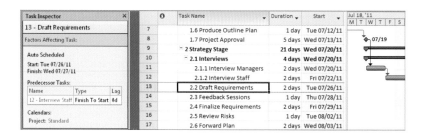

In the example above, the task inspector panel displays the name, start and finish dates of the selected task. It also contains details of the predecessor task(s), the dependency type, any lag time and the calendar(s) that are applied. The predecessor task(s) and calendar(s) are active hypertext links (shown in blue).

2. Click on the predecessor task name to back-track to that task

3. Click on the calendar name to display the relevant resource or project calendar

4. Click on the arrow alongside Inspect on the View ribbon and the drop down menu illustrated below right gives some additional options

The three additional options will, if selected, result in indicators being flagged on all tasks where: there is a potential problem requiring action; there is a suggested improvement that could be made; or a problem warning has been ignored.

Task Notes

Task notes can be attached to any task, to record additional, free text information. You can add a task note to a task in Gantt chart view, or any other view where the task note function is active on the Task ribbon.

1 Select the task that you wish to add the task note to

2 Click the Notes function on the Task ribbon to open the Task Information dialog box at the Notes tab, as illustrated below

3 Type in your note and format it, if required, (using the format buttons above the typing area), then click OK to add the note to the task

4 Now pause your mouse pointer over the yellow note symbol in the Information box to display the note

5 To edit the note or add further text to it, just double-click the yellow note symbol in the information box. This will reopen the task information dialog box at the note

6 To delete a note, just delete all the note text in the task information dialog box

You can also access task notes text by double-clicking on the task name (or clicking Information on the Task ribbon and selecting the Notes tab).

Deadline Dates

Deadline dates can be set on a task to indicate a date by which the task must be completed. If, at any time, the task slips, so that it will not be completed by its deadline date, a warning indicator will be displayed in the information box for the task.

Deadline dates are for information only and do not have any impact on the scheduling process. They should not be confused with task constraints (dealt with in chapter 11), which can determine when a task will be scheduled. Deadline dates are set on the Advanced tab of the Task Information dialog box.

① In Gantt chart view, double-click on the task you want to set a deadline for and the Task Information dialog box will open

② Select the Advanced tab (as illustrated above), click on the down arrow beside Deadline, select your deadline date and click OK. The deadline is indicated by a green arrow symbol on the Gantt chart:

If the task slips past its deadline date, a warning indicator will be displayed in the Information field. If you position your cursor over the warning indicator, the details will be displayed:

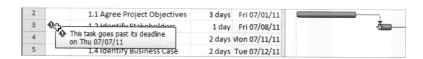

Moving Around

As your project starts to build up, you will soon reach a point where you will not be able to see all the project information in one view, particularly in Gantt chart view. As well as zooming in and out (which was covered in chapter 5), you will also need to be able to move around the view.

Scrollbars

You can use the scroll bars and sliders to move around vertically and horizontally. Gantt chart view has one vertical scrollbar (on the right-hand side of the screen), which moves the task sheet and the Gantt chart information up and down. It has two horizontal scroll bars (at the bottom of the screen), which move the task sheet and the chart left and right independently of each other.

Scroll To Task

When moving around with the scroll bars, it is quite easy to lose all sight of the Gantt chart part of the view. A useful short-cut is Scroll To Task, which will bring the appropriate part of the Gantt chart into view.

1 Click on the task(s) you want to bring into view in the task sheet and click Scroll To Task on the Task ribbon

The Gantt chart will scroll to bring the bar for the selected task(s) into view on the right-hand side of the screen.

You can use Ctrl+Home at any time to get back to the top left-hand corner of any view.

Critical Path

The Critical Path is the term given to the sequence of tasks that are critical to the duration of the project. A Critical Task is one that, if delayed or lengthened, will directly affect the project finish date.

The following diagram represents a simple project consisting of four tasks. Tasks A, C and D are each of one days' duration, while Task B is of two day's duration. Tasks B and C are both dependent on Task A, with finish-to-start relationships. Task D is dependent on both Tasks B and C, again with finish-to-start relationships. Assuming no lag time, the total duration of the project is four days.

Non-critical Tasks

Even if Task C was to slip by one day, it would still not impact the completion of Task D and, therefore, the project would still be completed in six days. Task C is, therefore, deemed to be a non-critical task.

Critical Tasks

On the other hand, if any of Tasks A, B or D were to slip by one day, the project would take five days to complete and these tasks are, therefore, deemed to be critical tasks.

Critical Path

The Critical Path is the path through the project that links all of the Critical Tasks. In the diagram above, the Critical Path (shown by the red line and red boxes) consists of Task A, the link between Task A and Task B, Task B, the link between Task B and Task D, and finally Task D.

Calculating the Critical Path

Calculating the critical path Project is done through the Critical Tasks function. This is covered in the next topic.

Critical Tasks

The critical path through the project is displayed using the Critical Tasks function on the Gantt chart Format ribbon. The default, when setting the critical path, is that critical tasks will be displayed in red and non-critical tasks in blue.

1   With your project in Gantt chart view, select the Format tab and click Critical Tasks

The critical path is calculated and the critical tasks are changed to red, as illustrated below:

2   To change the color (and any other details) of the critical task bars, select the down arrow beneath Format on the Gantt chart Format ribbon. Select Bar Styles from the drop down menu to open the Bar Styles dialog box, scroll down to select critical tasks and make any changes

Splitting Tasks

Normally, a task will be worked on from start to finish. But you can split a task if it needs to be interrupted and finished at a later time. Suppose that we have a task to Interview Managers and it needs to be split, as half of the managers are going to be on a conference the week it has been scheduled.

Hot tip

You will find this easier to do if you zoom in to make the task bars a reasonable size.

1 With your project in Gantt chart view, click on Split Task on the Task ribbon and a pop-up asks you to select the split point

11		2.1.1 Interview Managers	2 days	Wed 07/20/11	
12		2.1.2 I...			
13		2.2 Draft	Split Task:		
14		2.3 Feed	Scheduled Start:		
15		2.4 Finalize Requirements	Click to insert a split on the task.	2 days	Fri 07/25/11

2 Position the pointer on the task bar where you want to make the split (the pop-up will show the date where the split will start, as in the example above) and click. The task will then be split, with a 1 day gap

11		2.1.1 Interview Managers	2 days	Wed 07/20/11	
12		2.1.2 Interview Staff	2 days	Mon 07/25/11	
13		2.2 Draft Requirements	2 days	Wed 07/27/11	

3 You can now drag the right-hand part of the task bar, on the Gantt chart, to the right, to increase the gap (note that the cursor turns into a four-headed arrow, illustrated below, indicating that you can drag the task)

	🛈	Task Name	Duration	Start	Jul 18, '11	Jul 25, '11
					17 18 19 20 21 22 23 24	25 26 27 28 29 30
10		⊟ 2.1 Interviews	6 days	Wed 07/20/11		
11		2.1.1 Interview Managers	2 days	Wed 07/20/11		
12		2.1.2 Interview Staff	2 days	Tue 07/26/11		
13		2.2 Draft Requirements	2 days	Thu 07/28/11		
14		2.3 Feedback Sessions	1 day	Mon 08/01/11		

4 To remove a split, just drag the right-hand piece of the task bar back, so that it joins the left-hand piece again

	🛈	Task Name	Duration	Start	Jul 18, '11	Jul 25, '11
					17 18 19 20 21 22 23 24	25 26 27 28 29 30
10		⊟ 2.1 Interviews	4 days	Wed 07/20/11		
11		2.1.1 Interview Managers	2 days	Wed 07/20/11		
12		2.1.2 Interview Staff	2 days	Fri 07/22/11		
13		2.2 Draft Requirements	2 days	Tue 07/26/11		

Moving Linked Tasks

In the previous topic, we dragged part of a split task to move it backwards or forward in time. We can do the same thing with any task, but, if the task is linked, it may cause a scheduling conflict. In the following example, we will move the task after the split task back, to use the available time.

	ⓘ	Task Name	Duration	Start	Jul 18, '11 17 18 19 20 21 22 23 24	Jul 25, '11 25 26 27 28 29 30
10		⁻ 2.1 Interviews	6 days	Wed 07/20/11		
11		2.1.1 Interview Managers	2 days	Wed 07/20/11		
12		2.1.2 Interview Staff	2 days	Tue 07/26/11		
13		2.2 Draft Requirements	2 days	Thu 07/28/11		

1 Position your cursor over the task bar of the task you want to move (the cursor will turn into a 4-headed arrow), then drag the task bar back to where you want it to start and release the mouse key

2 If a planning wizard appears (as illustrated right), select Remove the link and click OK. The task will be unlinked and moved to where you dragged it (Cancel will undo the move)

3 Re-link the tasks as appropriate. In the example below, the moved task 2.1.2 stayed linked to the following task 2.2, so the preceding task 2.1.1 (which had lost its link in step 2) has also been linked to the following task 2.2

	ⓘ	Task Name	Duration	Start	Jul 18, '11 17 18 19 20 21 22 23 24	Jul 25, '11 25 26 27 28 29 30
10		⁻ 2.1 Interviews	4 days	Wed 07/20/11		
11		2.1.1 Interview Managers	2 days	Wed 07/20/11		
12	▦	2.1.2 Interview Staff	2 days	Thu 07/21/11		
13		2.2 Draft Requirements	2 days	Tue 07/26/11		
14		2.3 Feedback Sessions	1 day	Thu 07/28/11		
15		2.4 Finalize Requirements	2 days	Fri 07/29/11		

Note that, in the example above, the moved task is no longer on the critical path, so it has turned blue. There is also a calendar symbol in the task information box. If you position your cursor over the calendar symbol, it will display a note that the task has a 'start no earlier than' constraint.

Hot tip

Constraints are covered in chapter 11.

Summary

- Lag Time and Lead Time are used to create gaps (lag time) and overlaps (lead time) between tasks. The lag or lead time is indicated by the length of the line linking the two tasks on the Gantt chart

- Task Inspector allows you to view the constraints, dependencies and calendars that impact a task's start date, and you can follow these links to investigate any issues

- Task notes can be attached to any task and are indicated by a note symbol in the task's information box. They can be read, amended and deleted by double-clicking the note symbol or by double-clicking the task name and selecting the Note tab

- Deadline dates can be attached to any task that has a deadline. While they do not affect the scheduling, they will trigger a warning in the task information box if the task slips and is going to miss the deadline

- Moving around the Gantt chart can be done using the scroll bars, but the Scroll To Task function provides a useful shortcut for getting a task's task bar into view

- Another useful shortcut is Ctrl+Home, which will move to the top left-hand corner of the task sheet

- A critical task is one that will, if delayed, delay the final completion of the project. The Critical Path is the path through the project that links all the critical tasks

- Critical Tasks is the function, in Project, that is used for setting (or removing) the critical path

- The format of the critical path can be changed by using the Gantt chart Format ribbon

- Splitting a task allows the task to be split into two (or more) sections, with gaps of any required duration between them

- Tasks can be moved by dragging their task bar on the Gantt chart. If the task is linked, however, this may lead to a scheduling conflict. The best way to deal with this is to remove the link causing the conflict, move the task and then re-link it as required

7 Resources

Up to now we have dealt with planning a project and defining the tasks needed to carry it out. This chapter introduces project resources and the allocation of work to them.

84	Resource Sheet
85	Resource Information
86	Material & Cost Resources
87	Resource Notes
88	Assigning Resources
89	Multiple Resources
90	Team Planner
92	Timeline
94	Summary

Resource Sheet

Resources represent the human (people), material and financial resources you will use on your project. Resource Sheet view is where you enter details of these resources. It is called a sheet as it functions in a similar way to a spreadsheet. It can be accessed by selecting Resource Sheet on the View ribbon, or from the drop-down list of built in views from the Task ribbon.

 To enter a person, click in a blank Resource Name field, input the name of the resource and hit the Enter key

The Type defaults to Work (human resource), the Max Units to 100% (the full resource available to the project) and the Base Calendar to Standard. Costs are dealt with in the next chapter and, initially, it is best to leave these defaults as they are.

 Add the person's Initials, and Group, if required, and then add in the other people resources, as in the following example

	❶	Resource Name	Type	Material	Initials	Group
1		Prudence Project	Work		PP	PM
2		Joe Soap	Work		JS	Marketing
3		Mary Dee	Work		MD	Finance
4		Wendy Page	Work		WP	IT
5		Bill Buggs	Work		BB	Exec

You can change any details by selecting the field and editing it. You can add new resources to the end of the resource sheet or insert new resources in the middle (click on the resource you wish to insert the new resource in front of and press the Insert key).

You can also delete a resource by clicking on the Resource ID (the number on the left-hand side of the sheet) and pressing Delete.

Hot tip

The Group field does not have to be used for a group or department, you can use it for anything you want to be able to extract information on.

Resource Information

In addition to inputting information into the Resource Sheet, you can add additional resource information through the Resource Information dialog box.

 In Resource Sheet view, select the name of the resource you wish to add additional information for and click Information, from the Resource ribbon, to open the Resource Information dialog box, as illustrated below

Information

 On the General tab, you can change any of the information you input to the Resource Sheet and also add information about email address' and availability

In the example above, Joe is not going to be available for the project until September and he will then only be available for 50% of the time.

The other fields on the General tab are Windows Account (to look up someone on your network); Booking Type (Committed or Proposed, if someone is only provisionally allocated); Generic (for a resource type where there may be a team of people providing the work); Budget (for financial resources); Change Working Time (access to their calendar); and Details (to look up their details from your Outlook address book). Where relevant, these fields are dealt with in later topics.

Material & Cost Resources

In addition to work resources (people), you can also put in material resources (for consumable materials or supplies) and cost resources (where the cost is not dependant on the work or duration of a task).

1 Open your project in Resource Sheet view and add in any material resources you will be using

	ⓘ	Resource Name ▾	Type ▾	Material ▾	Initials ▾	Group ▾	Max. ▾
1		Prudence Project	Work		PP	PM	100%
2		Joe Soap	Work		JS	Marketing	0%
3		Mary Dee	Work		MD	Finance	100%
4		Wendy Page	Work		WP	IT	100%
5		Bill Buggs	Work		BB	Exec	100%
6		Paint	Material	gallon		Facilities	
7		Carpet	Material	sq metre		Facilities	

Note that, in the above illustration, Joe Soap has 0% Max Units. This is the result of changing his availability in the previous topic. It will show 0% until September, then it will show 50%.

2 Select a material resource and click on the Resource Information function on the Resource ribbon (note that, on the General tab, the work-related fields are deselected as they do not apply to material resources)

3 Select the Costs tab and input the cost: Standard Rate (used where the cost is dependant on the quantity used) and Per Use Cost (a one-off cost for using the resource)

Cost Resources

Cost resources are the third type of resource and they are used for costs that are unrelated to the work effort or the duration of a task. This would typically be for costs like travel or expenses that could be applied to a number of different tasks. Cost resources are dealt with in the next chapter.

Resource Notes

Resource Notes can be attached to resources in a similar manner to attaching task notes to tasks.

1. Select the Resource Name of the resource you want to attach the note to, click Notes on the Resource ribbon and the Resource Information dialog box opens at the Note tab, as illustrated below

2. Type in your note, format it if required, and click OK. The resource sheet now shows a note symbol in the Resource Information Box, as illustrated below

3. Position your cursor over the note symbol to display the note, as illustrated above

The note can be edited by double-clicking on it and making any required changes. It can be deleted by double-clicking on it and deleting all the text. It can also be accessed by opening the Resource Information dialog box and selecting the Notes tab.

Assigning Resources

Assigning resources is the process of allocating resources to tasks so that they can carry them out.

1 In Gantt chart view, select the task you wish to assign a resource to and click Assign Resources on the Resource ribbon (or press Alt+F10)

2 When the Assign Resources dialog box opens, select the Resource Name of the resource you wish to assign to the task and then click the Assign button

3 You can check a resource availability by selecting their name and clicking on the Graph button, which will display their work load as a graph in another pane below the Gantt chart

Once resources have been assigned to tasks, the Gantt chart will display the names of the resources allocated to each task, as in the illustration below. Where resources have been allocated at 100% (the default), no percentage is shown on the Gantt chart. But, if any resource is allocated at any other percentage, it is displayed after their name (as illustrated on task 1.3 below).

Multiple Resources

In many cases, you will just be assigning a single resource to each task (which is the best way of controlling a project). However, sometimes you may need to assign two or more resources to tasks.

1 Select the task you want to assign multiple resources to and then click Assign Resources on the Resource ribbon

2 Select the first Resource Name in the Assign Resources dialog box and click the Assign button (the resource will be assigned as in the previous topic)

3 Now select and assign the second resource

Hot tip

Hold down the Ctrl key in the Assign Resources dialog box to select more than one resource at one time.

Both resources are now allocated to the task, but note that a warning symbol has been placed in the task information box. When we added the second resource, Project needs to know how we want this interpreted.

4 Click on the warning symbol to display the options, as illustrated below

You've added new resources to this task. Is it because you wanted to:

○ Reduce duration so the task ends sooner, but requires the same amount of work (person-hours)

◉ Increase total work because the task requires more person-hours. Keep duration constant.

○ Reduce the hours that resources work per day. Keep duration and work the same.

Show me more details.

5 Select the first option to reduce the task duration, the second to keep the original duration or the third option to reduce the hours each will work

6 Select Show me more details (the fourth option) to open a help dialog box and select Using Resources and Adding Resources for more help

Team Planner

Team Planner is a new resource assignment view introduced in Project Professional 2010. It provides a drag and drop facility to simplify the assignment of tasks to resources, and the changes of assignments between resources.

 Select Team Planner from the Resource ribbon or from the drop down list of built in views

The upper part of the view displays the project resources with the tasks assigned to them. Overallocated resources are highlighted in red. Any unscheduled tasks will be displayed to the left of the Gantt chart. The lower part of the view displays the unassigned tasks.

2 Hover over a task to display the task level details, as illustrated on the right

3 Double click on a task to open the task details dialog box, or a resource to open the resource details dialog box

4 Select Details on the Resource ribbon to split the view and display a resource form in the bottom of the view, as illustrated at the top of the page opposite

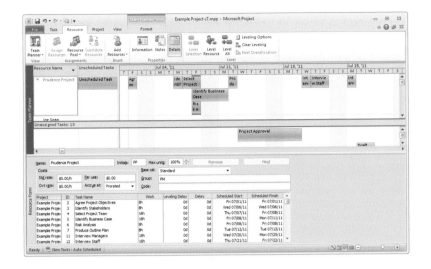

The resource form displays all the tasks allocated to the selected resource, as illustrated above.

5 To reallocate a task, simply drag it from its existing resource line and drop it onto the resource you wish to assign it to

In the illustration above, a task has been dragged from the location shaded in red in the top resource and dropped into the bottom resource. If this reassignment causes any conflicts, Project will display warnings and advice on the options for resolving them. Unallocated tasks can be assigned in a similar manner:

6 Drag any unassigned tasks from the lower part of the team planner and drop them onto the required resource in the upper part of the team planner

Timeline

Timeline is another new feature introduced in Project 2010. It provides a simple to use, high-level, graphic display of the project timeline. The timeline can be copied to an email or any other office document.

1 To display the timeline in Gantt chart view, select Timeline on the View ribbon

2 You can now specify the details you want displayed on the timeline, using Existing Tasks on the Format ribbon

3 Select the detail required from the dialog box (for this example, the project stages have been selected)

4 Click OK to update the timeline with the selected details

Formatting the Timeline

The Timeline Format ribbon contains functions for changing text styles and fonts, together with other formatting functions:

1 To improve the look of the timeline above, select each stage in turn and give it a different background color and appropriate text color, using the font group functions as illustrated below

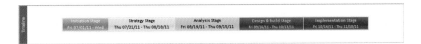

2 Use the Text Styles function to change the overall look of the text and annotations

3 Use Add Existing Task from the Format ribbon to add an existing milestone (as illustrated above) and insert new tasks, new milestones or new call out tasks, using the other functions from the Format ribbon

4 Use Copy Timeline from the Format ribbon to copy to email or other office application

Summary

- Project resources represent the people or human resources (Work), material resources (Material) and financial resources (Cost) you will use on your project

- Resource sheet view is the best place to input the basic details for your people and other project resources

- The resource information dialog box allows you to edit and add further resource information, including availability and working time

- Material resources can be used to allocate facilities and materials to the project, together with their costs. Material costs can be per unit costs or per use costs

- Cost resources can be used to record costs that are unrelated to the work effort or duration of a task. They are typically used for travel and other expenses

- Resource notes can be added to any resource and show up as a note symbol in the resource information box. Notes can be edited or deleted by double-clicking the note symbol

- Resources are assigned to tasks in Gantt sheet view, using the Assign Resources function on the Resource ribbon. Once assigned, they will be displayed on the Gantt chart

- Multiple resources can be assigned to a task and you can then select whether Project should reduce the duration of the task, increase the work effort or reduce the hours worked on the task

- Team Planner (only available in Project Professional) allows you to view assigned and unassigned tasks by resource, and allocate and re-allocate work between resources using the drag and drop functionality

- Timeline provides a simple to use, high-level, graphic display of your project timeline, which can be edited to show any required level of detail

- Project timelines can also be formatted and copied to email or any other office application for communication purposes, and they can be edited further in those applications

8 Project Costs

This chapter looks at adding revenue and fixed cost information to resources, tasks and assignments in order to build up the project budget.

96	Project Costs
97	Resource Costs
98	Fixed Costs
99	Variable Resource Costs
100	Cost Rate Tables
101	Applying Resource Rates
102	Cost Resources
104	Summary

Project Costs

Project costs fall into the general headings of: internal people costs, external people costs, other project costs and capital costs. All of these can be dealt with in Project. The ongoing revenue costs of operating the results of the project are not normally treated as project costs.

Project treats costs under two headings: Resource Costs (costs related to the people, material or cost resources you will use on the project) and Fixed Costs (not related to resource usage).

Resource Costs

Once you have identified all the stages, tasks and subtasks for a project, you will have estimated the work effort required to carry out the project. This should include the appropriate element of contingency (to deal with the unknown), based on where you are in the project. By adding resource costs for all the internal people who will be working on the project, Project will calculate all the people-related costs for you. Then you need to identify any external people costs (such as consultants, auditors, etc.) and feed those in as well.

When you have dealt with all the people related costs, then identify any material resource costs if your project is using costed material (such as paint or other types of consumables). Finally, any cost resources, which would cover travel, accommodation, training or other similar costs.

Fixed Costs

Once you have the internal and external people and material resource costs, you then need to identify any internal non-staff costs, such as any one-off charges for the use of facilities, rooms, computer usage, etc.

Finally, you will need to identify any other external capital or revenue costs, such as software package purchase, software development, equipment purchase or lease costs, and any other items of external expenditure.

All of these costs can be input into Project as Resource Costs or Fixed Costs on an appropriate task.

We will now work through each of these cost types and use the remaining topics in this chapter to see how they are treated in Project.

Resource Costs

Costs can be applied to resources or tasks and, typically, you will use resource costs for people on the project. Resource costs are normally shown as an hourly rate, which represents their salary plus overheads (that is their real cost to the business). Your organization may do things differently, so follow whatever their procedure is to calculate the appropriate hourly rates. The easiest way to allocate costs to resources is in the Resource Sheet.

1 Open the Resource Sheet by selecting Resource Sheet from the View ribbon

Hot tip

If any resources are highlighted in red, it indicates a resource conflict (this is dealt with in chapter 11).

97

2 Enter the appropriate hourly standard rate (and overtime rate if appropriate) for each resource, as illustrated below

	O	Resource Name	Type	Material	Initials	Group	Max.	Std. Rate	Ovt. Rate	Cost/Use
1	◈	Prudence Project	Work		PP	PM	100%	$40.00/hr	$50.00/hr	$0.00
2	✎	Joe Soap	Work		JS	Marketing	0%	$50.00/hr	$60.00/hr	$0.00
3		Mary Dee	Work		MD	Finance	100%	$30.00/hr	$35.00/hr	$0.00
4		Wendy Page	Work		WP	IT	100%	$35.00/hr	$40.00/hr	$0.00
5		Bill Buggs	Work		BB	Exec	100%	$60.00/hr	$60.00/hr	$0.00
6		Paint	Material	gallon		Facilities		$12.50		$0.00
7		Carpet	Material	sq metre		Facilities		$24.98		$0.00
8		Travel	Cost			T & E				
9		Accomodation	Cost			T & E				
10		Training	Cost			T & E				

3 If a resource has a one-off cost for each use (such as hire of a meeting room), enter the cost in the Cost/Use field

4 Finally, there is also a resource type of Cost (used for travel, accommodation and training in the above example), which can be used to assign arbitrary costs to tasks, so the actual amount will need to be entered for each usage

Hot tip

Cost resources are fully explained later in this chapter (pages 102-3).

Fixed Costs

Fixed costs are used when a task has a fixed cost associated with it, rather than the cost being associated with the resource. In the following example, we are going to add the cost of purchasing a computer software package to the task Purchase Software.

1 In Gantt chart view, select Tables from the View ribbon and then select Cost from the drop down built in menu (as illustrated on the right)

The cost columns will be added to the task table, replacing the previous task Entry columns (as illustrated in the example below)

	Task Name	Fixed Cost	Fixed Cost Accrual	Total Cost	Aug 22, '11	Aug 29, '11	Sep 05, '11
1	+ 1 Initiation Stage	$0.00	Prorated	$4,640.00			
9	+ 2 Strategy Stage	$0.00	Prorated	$4,160.00			
20	− 3 Analysis Stage	$0.00	Prorated	$14,800.00			
21	3.1 Agree Requirements	$0.00	Prorated	$1,600.00	Prudence Project		
22	3.2 Select Software Package	$0.00	Prorated	$1,600.00		Prudence Project	
23	3.3 Purchase Software	$10,000.00	Prorated	$11,600.00			
24	3.4 Contingency	$0.00	Prorated	$0.00			
25	− 4 Design & Build Stage	$0.00	Prorated	$0.00			

2 Type the estimated fixed cost for the task into the Fixed Cost field, as illustrated above

In this example, there is a resource allocated to the task and, therefore, the total cost of the task includes the fixed cost plus the resource cost (40 hours at $40 per hour). The other fields in the task cost table are baseline, actual, variance and remaining, as illustrated below.

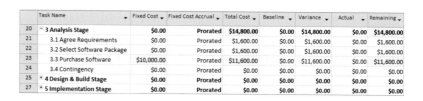

	Task Name	Fixed Cost	Fixed Cost Accrual	Total Cost	Baseline	Variance	Actual	Remaining
20	− 3 Analysis Stage	$0.00	Prorated	$14,800.00	$0.00	$14,800.00	$0.00	$14,800.00
21	3.1 Agree Requirements	$0.00	Prorated	$1,600.00	$0.00	$1,600.00	$0.00	$1,600.00
22	3.2 Select Software Package	$0.00	Prorated	$1,600.00	$0.00	$1,600.00	$0.00	$1,600.00
23	3.3 Purchase Software	$10,000.00	Prorated	$11,600.00	$0.00	$11,600.00	$0.00	$11,600.00
24	3.4 Contingency	$0.00	Prorated	$0.00	$0.00	$0.00	$0.00	$0.00
25	+ 4 Design & Build Stage	$0.00	Prorated	$0.00	$0.00	$0.00	$0.00	$0.00
27	+ 5 Implementation Stage	$0.00	Prorated	$0.00	$0.00	$0.00	$0.00	$0.00

Variable Resource Costs

It is quite possible that resource costs may change during the course of a project. For example, someone may receive a promotion or salary increase for doing such a good job on the project. Any changes to resource costs should be entered using the Resource Information dialog box.

1 In resource sheet view, select the Resource Name of the resource to be changed, click Information on the Resource ribbon to open the Resource Information dialog box and select the Costs tab

2 On the A (Default) tab, click in the next available Effective Date (below any existing cost information) and use the drop-down arrow to select the date for the new rate

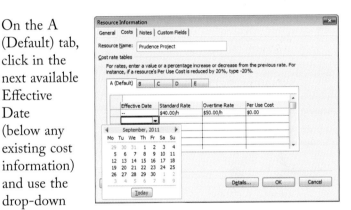

3 Enter new Standard and Overtime rates that will be effective from this date and then click OK

These new cost rates will become effective on all work from the effective date onwards. All work before that effective date will still be costed at the existing rate. If required, you can input up to 24 changes of resource costs for each resource.

Don't forget

You can also double-click on the Resource Name to open the Resource Information dialog box.

Hot tip

You can also put in a percentage figure for an increase or a negative percentage for a decrease.

Cost Rate Tables

In addition to being able to change cost rates, Project will also allow you to set up tables of rates for a resource. This can be useful if you need to use different cost rates for different types of work for the same person.

The cost rate tables are selected in the Costs tab in the Resource Information dialog box.

1 In resource sheet view, double-click on a Resource Name to open the Resource Information dialog box

2 Select the Costs tab at the top and then click on tab B in the middle Cost rate tables area, as illustrated

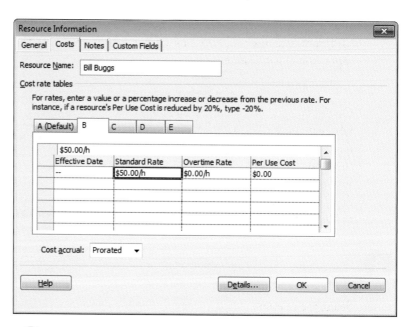

3 Type in the second standard rate (and overtime rate if it is required)

4 Enter the effective date, if relevant (see previous topic)

5 Add any further rates in tabs C, D and E, if required

6 Click OK to save the new rates table

Applying Resource Rates

Having set up a cost rates table, as in the previous topic, it can now be applied to any relevant tasks where this resource is allocated. Rate A will be used by default unless it is changed.

1 Select Task Usage from the View ribbon

	ⓘ	Task Name	Work	Details							Jul 11, '11
					W	T	F	S	S	M	
2		⊟ Agree Project Objectives	8 hrs	Work							
		Prudence Project	8 hrs	Work							
3		⊟ Identify Stakeholders	8 hrs	Work	8h						
		Prudence Project	8 hrs	Work	8h						
4		⊟ Select Project Team	32 hrs	Work		16h	16h				
		Prudence Project	16 hrs	Work		8h	8h				
		Bill Buggs	16 hrs	Work		8h	8h				
5	▥	⊟ Identify Business Case	16 hrs	Work							8h
		Bill Buggs	16 hrs	Work							8h

2 Identify the resource and task where you wish to apply a different rate and double-click on the Resource Name to open the Assignment Information dialog box

3 On the General tab, click on the down-arrow beside the Cost rate table to show the drop-down list of rates, as illustrated right

4 Select the relevant rate you wish to apply to this task and then click OK

Note that, in the example illustrated above, the new cost rate has now been applied and the cost of the work on this task has been recalculated at the new rate. This has reduced the rate from $60 to $50 per hour, so the cost of the 16 hours of work on this assignment has reduced from $960 to $800.

Cost Resources

In addition to Work (human) resources and Material resources, there are also Cost resources. These are used for types of costs other than fixed or capital costs. They are typically used for travel, accommodation and training costs. To use these cost resources, we first need to set them up in the Resource Sheet.

1 Open the Resource Sheet by selecting Resource Sheet from the View ribbon

2 Select a blank line and enter a name for the cost resource, as illustrated below

Note that Project automatically completes the default type, initials, max, charge rates and other information. This now needs to be changed:

3 Move to the resource type column and type cost or select it from the drop down list

Note that, in the previous illustration, once cost is selected as the resource type, several of the automatically completed fields are now cleared. In particular, the cost fields are blanked out. This is because we will be allocating the cost each time we use this resource.

4 Add in any further information and other cost resources, as in the following illustration

	❶	Resource Name ▼	Type ▼	Material ▼	Initials ▼	Group ▼	Max. ▼	Std. Rate ▼	Ovt. Rate ▼	Cost/Use ▼
8		Travel	Cost			T & E				
9		Accomodation	Cost			T & E				
10		Training	Cost			T & E				

Using Cost Resources

Cost resources are allocated to tasks in a similar way to work and material resources:

1 In Gantt chart view, select the task you wish to apply a cost resource to

	❶	Task Name ▼	Duration ▼	Start ▼	18, '11 19 20 21 22 23 24	Jul 25, '11 25 26 27 28 29 30 31	Aug 01, '11 01 02 03 04
9		⊟ 2 Strategy Stage	21 days	Wed 07/20/11			
10		⊟ 2.1 Interviews	4 days	Wed 07/20/11			
11		2.1.1 Interview Managers	2 days	Wed 07/20/11		Prudence Project	
12	⊞	2.1.2 Interview Staff	2 days	Thu 07/21/11	Prudence Project		
13		2.2 Draft Requirements	2 days	Tue 07/26/11		Prudence Project	

2 Select Assign Resources from the Resource ribbon to open the Assign Resources dialog box

3 Select the required cost resource, click Assign and then enter the budget cost for this task ($200 in the example). The cost resource and budget are then displayed on the Gantt chart, as illustrated below

	❶	Task Name ▼	Duration ▼	Start ▼	18, '11 19 20 21 22 23 24	Jul 25, '11 25 26 27 28 29 30 31	Aug 01, '11 01 02 03 04
9		⊟ 2 Strategy Stage	21 days	Wed 07/20/11			
10		⊟ 2.1 Interviews	4 days	Wed 07/20/11			
11		2.1.1 Interview Managers	2 days	Wed 07/20/11		Prudence Project,Travel[$200.00]	
12	⊞	2.1.2 Interview Staff	2 days	Thu 07/21/11	Prudence Project		
13		2.2 Draft Requirements	2 days	Tue 07/26/11		Prudence Project	

Summary

- Project can track budget and actual costs for internal and external people, material and other revenue cost items, together with capital costs

- Project differentiates between resource costs (costs associated with people, material or other cost resources) and fixed costs (such as equipment purchase) that are not resource-related

- Resource sheet is used for entering details of human resources (people), including standard and overtime hourly costs rates

- Details of material resource can also be entered in the resource sheet, with quantity costs or per use costs

- Details of cost resource can also be entered in the resource sheet, but, in their case, no cost details are entered as these are input when the resource is allocated to a task

- Fixed costs for capital or other fixed cost items can be input in Gantt chart view by applying the Cost table to the view in place of the normal entry table

- Resource cost can be varied through the life of the project, to reflect changes in salary, for example, by using the Costs tab in the Resource Information dialog box

- In addition to the default cost rate, four additional cost rates can be specified, if a resource is to be charged differently for different types of work. Again, these rates can be varied through the life of the project

- These additional (non-default) resource rates are best applied in the task usage view, using the Assignment Information dialog box

- Cost resources are set up in the resource sheet, as for other resource types, but no costs are entered for them

- When required, cost resources can be applied to a task using the assign resource dialog box and then the relevant amount can be entered in the dialog box

9 Project Calendars

This chapter explains what the various calendars are, how to set them up and assign and change them for individual resources and time-critical tasks.

106 Calendars

108 Project Defaults

109 Standard Calendar

110 New Base Calendar

111 Assigning a Calendar

112 Task Calendar

114 Resource Calendar

116 Summary

Calendars

The scheduling process consists of allocating tasks to resources, in line with their availability. So, the first step in scheduling is to know the availability and non-availability of the resources you will be using (e.g. when they are going to be on vacation, training or any other absences during the project).

Project uses calendars to determine working and non-working days, default start time and the working hours in a day. Calendars are automatically assigned to each work resource (person), but they can also be applied to tasks. So resources, tasks and calendars are all interlinked.

Tasks

Tasks determine the amount of work that needs to be carried out (the work effort), expressed as the total number of person/hours that need to be worked to complete the task. Until any resources are assigned to the task, Project assumes that a single resource (100%) will be allocated to it and schedules it on that basis.

Resources

Once a resource is allocated to a task, Project recalculates the duration (how many days it will take to complete), based on the amount of available resources allocated to it.

Calendars

Project then checks the resource calendar for each resource's availability and, if necessary, reschedules the task to take into account the availability of the resource. Finally, Project checks if a task calendar has been assigned to a task and, if so, also takes that into account when scheduling the task.

There are three types of calendar: base calendars, resource calendars and task calendars. Base calendars define the working days and hours for the whole project (or for a group of resources within the project). Resource calendars define the working days and working hours for each individual resource (person). Task calendars define when a task can or cannot take place.

The Standard calendar is the default project base calendar. It defines the working days and hours for the project. When a resource is added to a project, the standard calendar is allocated to that resource as its base calendar. Any changes to the standard calendar will be reflected in the dependant resource calendars.

There is a third element to this relationship, and that is the project defaults. These form the top-level of the relationship:

1 Project Defaults are set in the Project Options dialog box (illustrated below). This allows you to change the default working hours and hours in a working day, week and month. These are all used by Project in setting task durations and scheduling tasks

107

2 Base Calendars (as illustrated right) are based on the project defaults, but you can redefine the working hours in a day and in a week for the project. More importantly, you can also set any non-working days, such as public holidays

3 Resource Calendars are created for each resource and inherit their base calendar working days and hours. They are used to set annual vacation and other non working time. Task calendars are similar and can be created for any task that requires one

Project Defaults

Beware

Even if you don't work these hours, don't change the defaults unless you absolutely have to. It can make scheduling a real nightmare.

Project defaults are initially set so that working time is Monday to Friday, 8:00 AM to 12:00 PM and 1:00 PM to 5:00 PM. The standard calendar (see next topic) is also initially set to these working days and times.

Changing the defaults will change the way tasks are allocated, their duration and the way that resources are allocated to them. If you change the project defaults, it does not automatically change the standard calendar or any calendars based on it. So, if you do make changes to the defaults, you may also need to make changes to all your other calendars.

1. Select Options from the File tab to open the Program Options dialog box

2. Select Schedule from the menu on the left hand side (as illustrated below) to access the schedule options

3. Make any changes required to the project defaults

4. If you want the changes to apply to all new projects, click the drop down arrow beside your project name and select All New Projects, then click OK

5. If you have made any changes to the Default start time, Default end time, Hours per day or Hours per week, you will need to change the Standard calendar (and any other base calendars you have created) to bring them into line with the new defaults (see next topic)

Beware

If you change the Default hours per day after you have entered any tasks, the task durations will change, as they will still have the original hours as their work effort.

Standard Calendar

The standard calendar has the default working time set as 8:00 AM to 12:00 PM and 1:00 PM to 5:00 PM on Monday to Friday. If you have changed the project defaults, you will need to bring the standard calendar into line. You can then put in any public or other holidays that will apply to the whole project.

1 Select Change Working Time from Project ribbon to open the Change Working Time dialog box

2 The scroll bar on the right of the calendar changes the month. Click on a day to show its working time

3 To change all working times, select the Work Weeks tab, select Default and click the Details button

4 In the Details dialog box, select the days to change (Monday to Friday for the whole week), change the From time and To time as required and then click OK

5 To enter holidays, select the required month and day, click the Exceptions tab, enter the holiday name and click the Details button

6 In the Details dialog box, make the day non-working and click OK to save it

New Base Calendar

Project comes with three base calendars (standard, night shift and 24 hours) but, if none of these are suitable, you can create a new one from the project defaults or by copying an existing calendar.

1 Select Change Working Time from the Project ribbon and click Create New Calendar (top right-hand corner)

2 Name the new calendar and select if you want to start with a copy of an existing calendar

The new calendar will open in the Change Working Time dialog box and will inherit anything from the calendar you based it on.

3 Select the Work Weeks tab, select Default, click on the Details button to open the Details dialog box and enter details of your required From and To working times, as illustrated

This example is for a shift, so Monday would need to be 9:00 PM to 12:00 AM and Saturday 12:00 AM to 5:00 AM.

Don't forget

In Project, 12:00 AM is midnight and 12:00 PM is midday. If you select the 24-hour clock, 00:00 is midnight and 12:00 is midday.

Assigning a Calendar

Having set up your standard calendar and created any new base calendars, you can now assign them to the project team, as required. The standard calendar is assigned by default, the other base calendars can be assigned using the Resource Information dialog box or directly in Resource Sheet view.

Hot tip

If you have made changes to a resource calendar and then assign a new base calendar to the resource, the changes will be retained after the new base calendar has been applied.

1 In Resource Sheet view, double-click on the Resource Name of the person whose base calendar you wish to change to open the Resource Information dialog box

2 On the General tab, click the Change Working Time button (on the right) to open the Change Working Time dialog box for the resource

3 Click the down arrow beside Base calendar to get the drop down list of calendars, select the required base calendar and click OK. Click OK again to close the Resource Information dialog box

4 To assign a new base calendar directly in Resource Sheet view, click on the existing Base Calendar (on the right-hand side of the sheet) and select the required calendar from the drop down list

	Resource Name	Type	Material	Initials	Group	Max.	Std. Rate	Ovt. Rate	Cost/Use	Accrue At	Base Calendar
1	Prudence Project	Work		PP	PM	100%	$40.00/hr	$50.00/hr	$0.00	Prorated	Standard
2	Joe Soap	Work		JS	Marketing	0%	$50.00/hr	$60.00/hr	$0.00	Prorated	Standard
3	Mary Dee	Work		MD	Finance	100%	$30.00/hr	$35.00/hr	$0.00	Prorated	Standard
4	Wendy Page	Work		WP	IT	100%	$35.00/hr	$40.00/hr	$0.00	Prorated	
5	Bill Buggs	Work		BB	Exec	100%	$60.00/hr	$60.00/hr	$0.00	Prorated	24 Hours
6	Paint	Material	gallon		Facilities		$12.50		$0.00	Prorated	Special Calendar
7	Carpet	Material	sq metre		Facilities		$24.98		$0.00	Prorated	Standard
8	Travel	Cost			T & E					Prorated	

The new base calendar is applied to the resource in exactly the same way as using the Resource Information dialog box.

Task Calendar

If a task can only take place at a certain time and/or on certain days, this can be defined by assigning a task calendar to the task.

For example, it may be that a presentation to management must take place at a weekly management meeting, and these are always held on Friday mornings.

1 If necessary, split the task into the report preparation and the presentation (to isolate the presentation)

	ⓘ	Task Name	Duration	Start	'11	Aug 08, '11
					03 04 05 06 07	08 09 10 11 12 13
15		2.4 Finalize Requirements	2 days	Mon 08/01/11	Prudence Project	
16		2.5 Review Risks	1 day	Wed 08/03/11	Prudence Project	
17		2.6 Forward Plan	2 days	Thu 08/04/11	Prudence Project	
18		**2.7 Report to Management**	**1 day**	**Mon 08/08/11**		
19		2.7.1 Prepare Report	0.5 days	Mon 08/08/11		
20		2.7.2 Present to Management	0.5 days	Mon 08/08/11		
21		2.8 Contingency	8 days	Tue 08/09/11		

112

2 Create a new base Management Meeting calendar (as a copy of Standard) and click OK

3 The change working time dialog box will open at the new calendar. Select Default on the Work Weeks tab and click the Details button

4 Select Monday to Thursday on the left, then click on the Set days to the non-working time option on the right

5 Then select Friday on the left, Set days to specific times on the right, delete the afternoon From working time (this will also delete the afternoon To working time) to just leave Friday mornings as working time and then click OK twice to save this

We have now created a Management Meetings calendar with just Friday mornings as working time. We now have to assign it to the relevant task as a task calendar.

6 In Gantt chart view, double-click on the Present to Management task to open the Task Information dialog box, as illustrated below

7 On the Advanced tab, assign the new calendar (as illustrated above) and the task is rescheduled to the next available Friday morning:

	ⓘ	Task Name	Duration	Start	'11 / 03 / 04 / 05 / 06 / 07	Aug 08, '11 / 08 / 09 / 10 / 11 / 12 / 13
15		2.4 Finalize Requirements	2 days	Mon 08/01/11	Prudence Project	
16		2.5 Review Risks	1 day	Wed 08/03/11	Prudence Project	
17		2.6 Forward Plan	2 days	Thu 08/04/11	Prudence Project	
18		2.7 Report to Management	4.5 days	Mon 08/08/11		
19		2.7.1 Prepare Report	0.5 days	Mon 08/08/11		
20		2.7.2 Present to Management	0.5 days	Fri 08/12/11		
21		2.8 Contingency	8 days	Fri 08/12/11		

As the delay to the presentation to management has effectively put a 3.5 day lag time between preparing the report and presenting it to management, the tasks in front of it are no longer on the critical path (note that they have turned blue). They can slip by 3.5 days without impacting the project. Of course, the end of the project has just been put back as well (unless there is spare lag time further on in the project).

One final point to note is that a task calendar symbol has now been created in the task information box to warn us that this task has a calendar assigned to it.

Resource Calendar

Each resource is automatically assigned a resource calendar. This is initially based on the standard calendar, although a different base calendar can be assigned, if required. The resource calendar will inherit any holidays or project-wide variations, but it also needs to have resource-specific variations added, such as vacation or other non-working time and non-standard working hours.

Change Working Hours

Individual resources may well have non-standard working hours or may work part time. Both of these variations can be recorded in their resource calendar. Changes to working hours are entered through the Change Working Time dialog box.

1 Select Change Working Time from the Project ribbon to open the Change Working Time dialog box

2 At the top, select the resource you wish to change, select the Work Weeks tab and click the Details button on the right hand side to open the Details dialog box (see below right)

3 Select the days to change on the left and select Set days to these specific working times

4 Enter the new working hours for the resource and then click OK

Change Working Week

The working week for a resource can also be changed in the Change Working Time dialog box. For example, if a resource now only works Monday to Thursday:

1 Open the Details for the resource and select Friday

2 Click Set days to non-working time option and click OK

Vacations and Absences

Vacations and any other absences are also entered through Change Working Time.

1 Open the Change Working Time dialog box, select the resource for whom you wish to enter a vacation, or other absence, and click on the Exceptions tab (see below)

2 Click under Name on the Exception tab and enter a name for the absence

3 Select the Start and Finish dates using the drop down calendars in the Start and Finish columns

4 Enter any other absences, then click OK twice to save the changes and close the resource information dialog box

Summary

- When allocating a resource to a task and scheduling it, Project uses calendars to check the availability of that resource to carry out the task, and on any limitations on when the task can be performed

- Project defaults determine how Project will schedule work, base calendars are used to define project or group working times, while resource calendars are used to determine an individual resource's availability. Task calendars provide an option for determining when a time-critical task can be performed

- Project defaults specify the number of working hours in a day and a week, for scheduling purposes, and the default start and end time for a working day. They also define the first day of the week, the start of the fiscal year and the number of working days in a month

- The standard (project) calendar is the default base calendar for the project and is where project working time and non-working days are specified. It needs to be kept in step with the project defaults

- A new base calendar is best created based on the standard calendar, so that it inherits any project information

- The standard calendar is allocated to all resources by default, but any other base calendar can be allocated through the change working time dialog box or on the resource sheet

- Task calendars are used when a task can only happen at certain times. They are defined by limiting the working time and then allocated to a task through the task information dialog box

- Resource calendars are used to enter non-standard working hours for a resource and to change the working week (days worked)

- Resource calendars are also used to set the non-working time for each individual resource, by defining their vacations, training and other non-available times

10 Project Scheduling

This chapter deals with scheduling a project, and how the different task types and contouring affect that process. It also covers setting and clearing baselines and interim plans.

118 User Controlled Scheduling

119 Automatic Scheduling

120 Fixed Unit Tasks

121 Fixed Duration Tasks

122 Fixed Work Tasks

123 Resource Contouring

124 Task Contouring

126 Setting a Baseline

127 Interim Plans

128 Clearing a Baseline

129 Backward-Scheduling

130 Summary

User Controlled Scheduling

User controlled scheduling allows you to schedule tasks manually with whatever information you have available. It is the alternative mode to automatic scheduling, which will schedule tasks with calculated dates and durations. You can set either mode as the default and override the default for individual tasks.

1 To set the mode to manual scheduling, click on Mode on the Task ribbon and select Manually schedule from the drop down list. All new tasks will now be manually scheduled, but existing tasks will be unaltered

2 To change an existing, automatically scheduled task to manually scheduled, select the task and click on Manually Scheduled on the Task ribbon (as illustrated above)

3 To create a manually scheduled task, click Insert Task on the Task ribbon while in manually scheduled mode

4 Enter the task name (as illustrated below)

	ⓘ	Task Name	Duration	Start	Sep 19, '11	Sep 26, '11
					19 20 21 22 23 24 25	26 27 28 29 30 01
27		− 4 Design & Build Stage	20 days?	Wed 09/21/11		
28		4.1 Design Work				
29		4.2 Dummy Task	20 days	Wed 09/21/11		
30		+ 5 Implementation Stage	20 days	Wed 10/19/11		

5 You can now manually schedule the task by entering a duration and start date when known

6 You can also enter placeholder text in the duration and start fields (as illustrated below)

	ⓘ	Task Name	Duration	Start	Sep 19, '11	Sep 26, '11
					19 20 21 22 23 24 25	26 27 28
27		− 4 Design & Build Stage	20.5 days?	Wed 09/21/11		
28		4.1 Design Work	5 days	Wed 09/21/11		
29		4.2 Initial Build Work	n/a	October		
30		4.3 Dummy Task	20 days	Wed 09/21/11		
31		+ 5 Implementation Stage	20 days	Wed 10/19/11		

Automatic Scheduling

For automatic scheduling, Project uses the tasks, the resources allocated to them and the resource and task calendars to work out when tasks can be started, worked on and completed.

Forward-Scheduling

The default approach to scheduling is to forward-schedule from a start date. You can also backward-schedule from a finish date, although there are certain problems that can result from this (covered later in this chapter).

The way that the schedule will be affected when resources, work effort or durations change is also dependent on the scheduling method and task types. The scheduling method can be either effort-driven or not. Tasks can be of fixed unit, fixed duration or fixed work types. The default is fixed unit, non-effort-driven tasks, but we will look at examples of each of these types.

Effort-Driven Scheduling

With effort-driven scheduling turned off, adding an additional resource to a 2 day duration, fixed unit task will increase the work effort by 2 days to 4 days, but the duration will remain unchanged (as there are now two people doing it).

This can be changed to effort-driven scheduling in Project Options on the File tab. With effort-driven scheduling on, the duration of a task is adjusted to fit in with any changes to the resources. If a task is going to require 16 hours work effort and you allocate two resources to it (at 100%), it will be given a duration of 8 hours (1 day).

If you then remove one of the resources, the additional day's work will be reallocated to the remaining resource, so the duration will be extended to 2 days.

Task Types

The task type (fixed unit, fixed duration or fixed work) will determine what will be changed to accommodate any other changes. The basic equation used by Project is:

$$\textbf{Work = Duration x Units}$$

Where Work is the work effort required, Duration is how long it will take and Units are resources and their allocation percentage.

Fixed Unit Tasks

The fixed unit task is the default task type in Project. If resources are added to or removed from a task, the work effort or duration will be affected. In the following example, we will allocate a second resource to a task.

1 In Gantt chart view select Details from the View ribbon

2 In the above example, we have selected a 1 day task with a single resource assigned to it and 8 hours of work have been allocated to the resource in the (lower) task form

3 If we assign a second resource to the task (as illustrated below), the duration remains as 1 day with 8 hours work now allocated to each of the two resources

4 Click on the smart tag to change this, to reduce the duration to half a day with 4 hours work allocated to each of the resources, if that is what was required

Hot tip

Note that Effort driven is not selected in the Task From. If selected, the allocation of a second resource would reduce the duration rather than increase the work effort.

Fixed Duration Tasks

If a task is a fixed duration task, then (as the name implies) the duration remains fixed whether resources are added or removed. This has an impact on the way scheduling takes place, depending on whether effort-driven scheduling is being used or not.

Effort-Driven Scheduling

If effort-driven scheduling is being used, this means that adding another resource to an existing task will split the work between the two resources. The work effort will remain the same, the duration will remain the same, so their units will be reduced to 50% to balance that.

Non-Effort-Driven Scheduling

If effort-driven scheduling is not being used, this means that adding another resource to an existing task will double the work. The duration stays the same, the units will be 100%, so the work effort will double (an example of this follows).

1 Select a task with one resource allocated to it and, in the lower panel (task form), change the task type to Fixed Duration and deselect "Effort driven" if selected

2 Now, if a second resource is assigned to the task

The duration has stayed the same so the work effort has doubled to 32 hours. This is the type of task to use when duration stays the same regardless of the number of resources allocated.

Fixed Work Tasks

The third type of task is the fixed work task. A fixed work task must be effort-driven (as the amount of work is fixed), so only the duration and resource units can be affected. Adding another resource will reduce the duration, while increasing the duration will reduce the resource units.

1 Select a task with one resource assigned to it and, in the lower panel (task form), change the Task type to Fixed Work (note that "Effort driven" deselects so it cannot be changed) and click OK

2 Now, if a second resource is assigned to the task (as below), the work effort remains 8 hours (4 hours each) so the duration has reduced to half a day

3 Change the Duration back to 1 day and a smart tag appears asking if you want to increase the work effort or just make the task take longer (the default)

Resource Contouring

Project includes a feature that allows you to contour resource availability. This feature is aimed at situations where an individual is only available to a project part-time, with the percentage of their available time changing from period to period. Alternatively, it would be applicable if a team of people were going to be working on a task or set of tasks and the team were going to have varying numbers of people available over time (perhaps building up the team initially and then releasing them in a phased way).

1 In Resource Sheet view, double-click on the name of the resource you wish to contour to open the Resource Information dialog box

2 On the General tab, enter the Available From and To dates with the relevant Units (in the above example, the resource is only available 50% during August)

3 If this produces any conflicts with the scheduled work for this resource, the resource will be highlighted in red, with a warning symbol in the Resource Information box (see below). Conflicts are dealt with in the next chapter.

	🛈	Resource Name ▼	Type ▼	Material ▼	Initials ▼	Group ▼	Max. ▼
1		Prudence Project	Work		PP	PM	100%
2	◇	The resource is overallocated and should be leveled.			JS	Marketing	0%
3		Mary Dee	Work		MD	Finance	100%

Task Contouring

When you assign a resource to a task, the total work is spread evenly throughout the duration of the task. This is referred to as a flat contour, but there are a number of other contours that you can apply in Project.

Contours can be applied or changed in Task Usage or Resource Usage views. In the former, the resources are grouped by task; in the latter, tasks are grouped by resource. In both cases, the right-hand side of the screen displays the work values and is used to contour the work.

Contours are applied using the Assignment Information dialog box. There are eight preset contours available:

Flat
Work hours are distributed evenly through the task duration.

Back Loaded
The hours start low and ramp up towards the end of the task.

Front Loaded
The hours start at 100% at the start of the task and tail off towards the end.

Double Peak
The hours peak twice during the task duration.

Early Peak
The hours peak during the first quarter of the task duration.

Late Peak
The hours peak during the last quarter of the task duration.

Bell
The hours start and finish low and peak in the middle of the task duration.

Turtle
Similar to Bell, but the hours start and finish higher (i.e. there is less variation).

Once a contour has been applied to a task, any changes to the start or finish dates, the resources allocated or the duration will be applied using that contour.

Applying a Contour

To apply a contour in Resource Usage view (the process is exactly the same in Task Usage view):

1 Select a task that is at least 2 days long (contouring is only really practical on larger tasks)

O	Resource Name	Work	Add New Column	Details	T	F	S	S	M	T	W	T	F
1 ⬥	⁻ Prudence Project	244 hrs		Work	8h	8h			16h		8h		
	Agree Project Objectives	8 hrs		Work									
	Identify Stakeholders	8 hrs		Work	8h								
	Select Project Team	16 hrs		Work		8h			8h				
	Risk Analysis	8 hrs		Work					8h				
	Produce Outline Plan	8 hrs		Work							8h		
🔊	Interview Managers	16 hrs		Work									
	Interview Staff	16 hrs		Work									
	Draft Requirements	16 hrs		Work									

2 Double-click on the task name to open the Assignment Information dialog box and select the General tab, as illustrated

3 Click the down arrow beside Work contour, select the contour you wish to apply and then click OK (in the example above, Late Peak was selected)

O	Resource Name	Work	Add New Column	Details	T	F	S	S	M	T	W	T	F
1 ⬥	⁻ Prudence Project	244 hrs		Work	8h	1.2h			3.6h	7.2h	12h		8h
	Agree Project Objectives	8 hrs		Work									
	Identify Stakeholders	8 hrs		Work	8h								
🔊	Select Project Team	16 hrs		Work		1.2h			3.6h	7.2h	4h		
	Risk Analysis	8 hrs		Work							8h		
	Produce Outline Plan	8 hrs		Work									8h
🔊	Interview Managers	16 hrs		Work									
	Interview Staff	16 hrs		Work									
	Draft Requirements	16 hrs		Work									

The 16 hours work, in the example above, has now been contoured so that the hours build up slowly and peak late in the task. The larger the task, the more apparent the contouring. The late peak symbol has been inserted into the task information box to indicate that a contour has been applied to the task.

Try applying the other contour types (as listed opposite) to see their effects on a task.

Setting a Baseline

Once you have created your project schedule, allocated resources, resolved any conflicts, and are happy with the project schedule, you are ready to set a baseline.

A baseline represents a record of a set point in time where you have agreed and fixed your project schedule. Project can hold up to eleven baselines for each project, named Baseline (for the first one) and then Baseline 1 to Baseline 10.

The first baseline you set should contain the original schedule only; subsequent baselines will contain the current schedule, with any actual data up to that point.

When you set a baseline, the dates, times and other data are recorded for all tasks.

1 In Gantt chart view, select Set Baseline from the Project ribbon to open the Set Baseline dialog box (as illustrated right)

2 Select Set baseline and For: Entire project and click OK to save the baseline

Hot tip

Baselines 1 to 10 can also be selected in the Save Baseline dialog box, and previously saved baselines can be updated by saving them again.

3 Select Project Information from the Project ribbon to open the Project Information dialog box. Click the Statistics button to view the current, baseline and actual details for the project (as illustrated below)

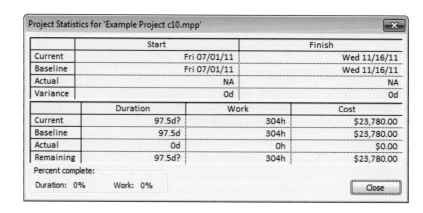

Project Statistics for 'Example Project c10.mpp'			
	Start		**Finish**
Current	Fri 07/01/11		Wed 11/16/11
Baseline	Fri 07/01/11		Wed 11/16/11
Actual	NA		NA
Variance	0d		0d

	Duration	Work	Cost
Current	97.5d?	304h	$23,780.00
Baseline	97.5d	304h	$23,780.00
Actual	0d	0h	$0.00
Remaining	97.5d?	304h	$23,780.00

Percent complete:

Duration: 0%   Work: 0%

Close

Interim Plans

As well as setting up to 11 baselines (which should be retained throughout the project), you can also create up to ten interim plans during the course of the project.

You may wish to create a new baseline at the end of each project stage, to reflect any changes to the project that have been agreed during that stage. But you may also wish to use interim plans to track more detailed changes to the project.

While a baseline saves a lot of information about a project, an interim plan just saves details of the current task start and end dates.

1 In Gantt chart view, select Set Baseline from the Project ribbon to open the Set Baseline dialog box

2 Select Set interim plan, select Copy: Scheduled Start/Finish, select Into: Start 1/Finish 1, select For: Entire project and click OK

3 As the project progresses, you can copy into Start 2/Finish 2 and so on

4 You can also update any existing interim plans by copying new information over the information previously saved

5 If you want to save interim plans for just the current stage of the project, select the tasks in the Gantt chart before opening the Save Baseline dialog box, then select For: Selected tasks instead of For: Entire project in Step 2 (above)

Interim plans are very useful for tracking changes made during a project stage. Then, at the end stage review, you will be able to look back and see what was changed and when. They can also be used for tracking changes during the whole project and used as part of the end project review, but, in practice, baselines are probably more suitable for this.

Clearing a Baseline

As well as updating baselines and interim plans, you can also clear them for the whole project, or for selected tasks.

1 Select Set Baseline on the Project ribbon and then select Clear Baseline to open the Clear Baseline dialog box

2 Select Clear baseline plan, select For: Entire project (as illustrated above) and click OK to clear the baseline

3 Select Project Information on the Project ribbon and click the Statistics button to confirm the baseline has gone

4 To clear selected tasks, first select the task names in Gantt chart view

5 Select Set Baseline from the Project ribbon and then Clear Baseline to reopen the Clear Baseline dialog box

6 Select Clear interim plan, select Start 1/Finish 1, select Selected tasks and click OK

Backward-Scheduling

The default method of scheduling is forward-scheduling from the project start date. This is what we have been using in all the examples so far. However, there may be times when you have to complete a project by a certain date. By scheduling backwards from a finish date, you can see when a project has to start. However, there is a right and a wrong way to go about this.

The Right Way

Use backward-scheduling right from the start. When you first create your project, set it to schedule back from the required completion date before you input any tasks:

1. Create a new project and select Project Information from the Project ribbon. Select Schedule from: Project Finish Date, enter the required finish date for the project and click OK

Then, as you input your tasks and allocate resources, Project will correctly backward-schedule your project. But what if you start off with forward-scheduling and then decide you need to switch to backward-scheduling?

The Wrong Way

Project will allow you to change from forward-scheduling to backward-scheduling, but it doesn't always work out too well. So make sure you save your project file before trying this.

1. Open your project in Gantt chart view, select Show Outline Level 1 and select Entire project from the View ribbon, to get the whole project into view

2. Select Project Information from the Project ribbon, change Schedule from: to Project Finish Date, enter the required finish date and click OK

3. Accept any warnings and carry on until the project has been rescheduled

Sometimes this works and sometimes it doesn't. If it worked, save the project with a new name. If it didn't work, you may have to start again by creating a new project (the right way).

Beware

Scheduling back from a finish date is more difficult and should be avoided until you have some experience of forward-scheduling.

Summary

- User controlled scheduling allows you to schedule tasks manually and leave part of the scheduling information blank, or with text placeholders for later completion

- Automatic scheduling involves Project taking the tasks, the resources allocated to them, and the resource calendars to work out the best time for each task to start and finish

- Work is the effort that will be required to complete a task (usually expressed in hours), duration is the length of time it will actually take (usually measured in days), and units are the resources that will be used to complete a task (expressed as a percentage, where 100% = one full resource)

- Fixed unit tasks are the default, where the units (resource percentage) remain constant and duration or work effort changes according to the number of resources allocated

- Fixed duration tasks with effort-driven scheduling will split the work between the resources, if more resources are added. With non-effort-driven scheduling, it will increase the work if more resources are added

- Fixed work tasks will only adjust duration and resource units, so adding a resource will reduce the resource percentage

- After a change, you can over-ride the way Project has rescheduled by using the smart tag in the task information box

- Resource contouring is the process of applying a different availability (unit percentage) over a series of time periods

- Contouring is the process of ramping work on a task up and down, and there are seven contour profiles that can be applied in addition to flat (the default)

- Baselines and interim plans represent snapshots of the project schedule at set points in time. They can be set, cleared and updated (replaced)

- Backward-scheduling is an option in Project but, if it is to be used, it should be used from the start of the project, if at all possible

11 Conflicts and Constraints

This chapter deals with resource conflicts and using leveling to resolve them. It also introduces task constraints, project calculation and moving a project.

132 Resource Conflicts

134 Resource Leveling

136 Manual Adjustment

138 Task Constraints

139 Applying Constraints

140 Constraint Conflicts

141 Viewing Constraints

142 Calculate Project

143 Move Project

144 Summary

Resource Conflicts

As you begin to assign resources to tasks and then make subsequent changes to tasks and schedules, you may begin to get resource conflicts. A resource conflict is where a resource is scheduled to perform more work than it can carry out in the time available. Project flags these conflicts for you by highlighting the relevant resource information in red and flagging the tasks causing the overallocation. Project provides a number of tools and options for dealing with these:

1 In Gantt chart view, position your cursor over a flag

2 Right-click on the task to bring up the options (as illustrated right)

3 Select Reduce Work to reduce the work effort of the task and remove the overallocation

4 Select Increase Duration to remove the overallocation by extending the duration of the task

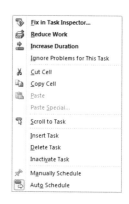

5 Select Ignore Problems for This Task to keep the overallocation but remove the flag

6 Select Fix in Task Inspector to open Task Inspector (as illustrated right)

Task Inspector displays the same options as listed above (the Ignore option being to de-select the tick at the bottom). It also displays additional information on the task, predecessor tasks, resource and reason for the overallocation.

In resource usage and other resource views, overallocated resources will be highlighted in red, as will the days on which overallocation occurs. Use Next Overallocation on the Resource ribbon to bring the overallocation into view (as illustrated below).

In the example above, the resource name on the summary line is highlighted in red, together with the Wednesday where we have created an overallocation of 20 hours. The details of the tasks are shown below the summary line, so that you can see exactly which tasks have caused the problem. The work can be adjusted in Team Planner (see page 90), if you have Project Professional, otherwise, Resource Allocation view provides some useful data.

Beware

Team Planner is not available in Project Standard.

7 Select View>More Views>Resource Allocation from the Resource ribbon and click the Apply button:

Now each overallocated task can be inspected in turn and the appropriate option selected for dealing with it (these options are covered in the next two topics). Use Next Overallocation to move on to the next overallocated task.

Resource Leveling

In Project, resource conflicts can be resolved either manually or automatically. The process used to resolve these conflicts is called resource leveling.

Always save your project before leveling, then, if anything goes wrong, you can get back to where you were.

1 Select View>More Views>Resource Allocation from the Resource ribbon and click the Apply button

2 Select Project Information from the Project ribbon and note the current project finish date

3 Select the lower (Leveling Gantt) panel so that it is active

4 Select Level Resource from the Resource ribbon to open the Level Resource dialog box (as illustrated right)

5 Select the resource (or resources by holding down the Ctrl key) that you wish to level and click the Level Now button

If you receive any warnings that Project cannot resolve some over-allocations, make a note of the dates and click on the Skip button to continue. You will need to deal with these by using manual adjustments (covered in the next topic).

Resource Leveling Issue

There are some issues with Project when carrying out resource leveling. In the example, we allocated our project manager to a task (2.2 Produce Draft Requirements) at 100%, so the 2 days work was scheduled as 2 days duration.

We then reduced the project manager's availability to 50% for August (on page 123), but it did not change the schedule (causing an overallocation). Now we have performed resource leveling, but Project cannot cope with this. It has scheduled the first day on July 29 (100% available) but then split the task and scheduled the second day on September 01 (when the resource is available 100% again). This is clearly not right, but we can fix it.

	Task Name	Duration	Start	August 2011	September 2011
11	2.1.1 Interview Managers	2 days	Mon 07/25/11	Prudence Project,Travel[$200.00]	
12	2.1.2 Interview Staff	2 days	Thu 07/21/11	Prudence Project	
13	2.2 Draft Requirements	2 days	Fri 07/29/11		Prudence Project
14	2.3 Feedback Sessions	1 day	Fri 09/02/11		Prudence Project,Bill Buggs

1 Select the task and click on Assign Resources on the Resource ribbon to open the Assign Resources dialog box

2 Select the resource and click the Remove button, then select the same resource and click the Assign button (the task is rescheduled for two days and flagged for the overallocation)

3 Now right-click on the overallocated task, select Increase Duration from the drop down list. The task is rescheduled to take three days (the first day at 100% and the next two at 50%, in line with the resource availability) and the overallocation flag is removed, as illustrated below

	ⓘ	Task Name	Duration	Start	Aug 01, '11	Aug 08, '11
12		2.1.2 Interview Staff	2 days	Thu 07/21/11		
13		2.2 Draft Requirements	3 days	Fri 07/29/11	Prudence Project	
14		2.3 Feedback Sessions	1 day	Wed 08/03/11	Prudence Project,Bill Buggs	
15		2.4 Finalize Requirements	2 days	Thu 08/04/11		
16		2.5 Review Risks	1 day	Mon 08/08/11		Pruden
17		2.6 Forward Plan	2 days	Tue 08/09/11		

Beware

This is a known issue and can be avoided if tasks are only allocated at a single rate of availability.

Manual Adjustments

In addition to using resource leveling to automatically resolve resource conflicts, you will also need to resolve some conflicts manually. This may be necessary if you do not want Project to extend the schedule, or (as in the previous topic) where Project cannot resolve the conflict.

Resolving a conflict manually can involve a number of options:

- Allocating more resources to a task

- Rescheduling or splitting a task

- Reallocating tasks to a different resource

- Adding overtime working

We will look at each of these in turn.

Allocating More Resources

To add additional resources to a task, select the task and click on Assign Resources from the Resource ribbon (see Fixed Unit Tasks on page 120 for an example).

Rescheduling a Task

The easiest way to reschedule a task that is causing an overallocation is to drag it to another time, when the required resource is available (see Moving Linked Tasks on page 81 for an example). When moving a linked task, you may receive Planning Wizard warnings (also covered on page 81) which necessitate removing links. So, following this rescheduling, you should re-link the moved task in an appropriate way.

In a similar way, we can split a task and move the split parts to times when the required resource is available (see Splitting Tasks on page 80).

Reallocating Tasks

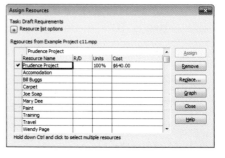

Select the task, click Assign Resources on the Resource ribbon to open the Assign Resources dialog box (as illustrated), click the Replace button and select the new resource from the list when prompted.

Don't forget

You can also reallocate tasks in Team Planner view if you have Project Professional.

Overtime Working

In addition to allocating more resources, rescheduling or reallocating a task, we can leave a task allocated where it is but complete it sooner by scheduling overtime working.

In the following example, let us say that we need to have task 4.1 (Design Work) completed as early as possible, and the resource assigned to it has agreed to work 2 additional hours (overtime) per day on this task.

	❶	Task Name	Duration	Start	Sep 19, '11							Sep 26, '11					
					18	19	20	21	22	23	24	25	26	27	28	29	30	01
27		4 Design & Build Stage	22.5 days	Mon 09/19/11													
28		4.1 Design Work	5 days	Mon 09/19/11				Prudence Project									
29		4.2 Initial Build Work	5 days	Mon 09/26/11													
30		4.3 Contingency	10 days	Wed 10/05/11													

1 Note the days that the task is being carried out

2 Select Change Working Time from the Project ribbon and select the appropriate resource calendar

3 Enter a description on the Exception tab and the Start and Finish dates

4 Click the Details button and enter the working time to include the 2 additional hours per day

	❶	Task Name	Duration	Start	Sep 19, '11							Sep 26, '11					
					18	19	20	21	22	23	24	25	26	27	28	29	30	01
27		4 Design & Build Stage	22.5 days	Mon 09/19/11													
28		4.1 Design Work	5 days	Mon 09/19/11				Prudence Project									
29		4.2 Initial Build Work	5 days	Fri 09/23/11													
30		4.3 Contingency	10 days	Wed 10/05/11													

Note that the duration of the task remains 5 days but the work is completed in less time, due to the 2 additional hours per day being worked by the allocated resource. The work is actually completed in four days, as can be seen on the Gantt chart above.

Task Constraints

When tasks are first entered into a project, they have the project start date as their start date (unless the project is backwards-scheduled, in which case, they have the project finish date as their finish date). As they are linked and have resources assigned to them, they will be scheduled depending on their dependencies and resource availability and be given their own start and finish dates.

Sometimes these allocated start and finish dates are not viable in the real world and a start or finish date has to be imposed. When this happens in Project, it is called setting a task constraint.

Task constraints are set in the form of: must start or finish on a particular date; start no earlier or later than a particular date; finish no earlier or later than a particular date; start as soon as possible; or finish as late as possible. The default constraint which is applied to all tasks on a forward-scheduled project is: start as soon as possible. For a backward-scheduled project, the default constraint is start as late as possible.

Constraints can also be flexible or inflexible. A flexible constraint is one where the project finish date can be moved by the task. An inflexible constraint is one where the project finish date cannot be moved by the task. The following table lists the flexible constraint types and any limitations on that flexibility:

Constraint	Flexible for
As Soon As Possible	All projects
As Late As Possible	All projects
Finish No Earlier Than	Forward-scheduled projects
Start No Earlier Than	Forward-scheduled projects
Finish No Later Than	Backward-scheduled projects
Start No Later Than	Backward-scheduled projects

The "As Soon As Possible" and "As Late As Possible" constraints do not use a date, while all the others have a date associated with them. The date is the earliest or latest date that the task can or must start or finish (as appropriate to the type of constraint).

Applying Constraints

The usual reason for applying a constraint to a task is that some internal or external factor means that it can only happen at a certain time. As an example, a good time to start using a new financial system is often the start of a new financial year. So, in this case, you might want to set a "start no earlier" constraint.

1 In Gantt chart view, select the task you wish to apply the constraint to and double-click on the Task Name to open the Task Information dialog box

2 Select the General tab and note the current start and finish dates for the task

3 Now select the Advanced tab, select the constraint type, set the constraint date, click OK and accept any warnings

In this example, we have set a constraint of Start No Earlier than January 01. The constraint is set, the schedule is adjusted and a constraint symbol is added to the task information box.

As usual, you can view the details of the constraint by positioning your pointer over the constraint symbol (as illustrated above). Note that, as this has effectively introduced a two and a half month lag time between this task and the preceding task, the earlier tasks are no longer on the critical path.

Hot tip

In practice, you would also want training to start as close as possible to the conversion date (a start "as late as possible" constraint would achieve this).

Constraint Conflicts

If you set a constraint that causes a conflict, the Planning Wizard appears to warn you of the problem and to offer suggestions for how you may be able to deal with it. As an example, we will force a constraint conflict by setting a "must finish on" constraint on task 2.7.2 Present to Management (below).

1 Double-click on the relevant task to open the Task Information dialog box and check the current dates in the General tab

2 On the Advanced tab, we will set a Must Finish On constraint, with the date of the preceding Friday

3 Click OK and the Planning Wizard will open, giving you a warning and offering you three options (as illustrated right)

4 Select the third option (to force the constraint), click OK, accept any further warning and the task will be rescheduled

In the example above, the task has been scheduled before three tasks it is dependant on are completed. You would not normally want to introduce this type of constraint conflict, so, in practice, you should select Cancel at step 4 and find another alternative.

Viewing Constraints

When a task has a constraint applied to it, there will be a constraint symbol in the task information box. The constraint symbol looks like a small calendar, and it will have a blue dot if it is a flexible constraint and a red dot if it is an inflexible constraint. If you pause your pointer over it, a pop-up will display details of the constraint.

1. In Gantt chart view, pause your pointer over a constraint symbol (the example on the right is the constraint set on the previous page)

You can also view constraints by applying the Constraints Dates table to the Gantt chart view.

2. Select Table>More Tables from the View ribbon to display the More Tables dialog box

3. Select Constraint Dates and click the Apply button to display the constraint details (as below)

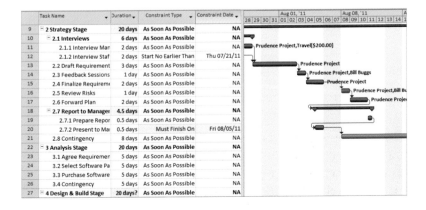

Calculate Project

By default, Project re-calculates the project schedule each time you make a change. You can suppress this and decide when you want Project to re-calculate and re-schedule the project.

1 Select Options from the File ribbon to open the Project Options dialog box

2 Select Schedule from the options list on the left hand side (as illustrated below)

3 Use the scroll bar on the right hand side to scroll down until you reach the Calculation section (as illustrated above)

4 Select the Off option to turn automatic calculation off and click OK

5 Once you have completed the changes to your project, select Calculate Project from the Project ribbon (as illustrated below) and the project will be re-scheduled

Move Project

Changing the project start will not automatically and correctly re-schedule every task in the project. This is due to the task dependencies and any constraints that have been applied. Project 2010 has introduced Move Project, a new feature which gets around this problem. It is also very handy if you want to use an old project as a template for a new one.

1 Open the old project, or the project that is to be moved, in Gantt chart view

2 Select Move Project from the Project ribbon (as illustrated above) and the Move Project dialog box opens

3 Select the new start date, select move deadlines (if the deadlines are to move in step) and click OK

The project is rescheduled and all dependencies and constraints are honoured wherever possible (as illustrated below). But it is worth scrolling through the whole project to check that no anomalies have crept in.

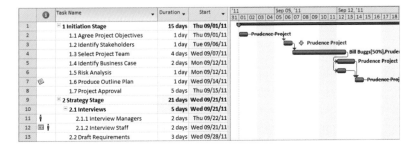

Summary

- Resource conflicts occur when the scheduled work cannot be carried out by the assigned resources in the required time frame

- Task Inspector provides useful help and guidance for dealing with these conflicts and there is a drop down menu available by right-clicking a task

- Project offers two options for resource leveling: manual (where you tell it when to level) and automatic (where leveling is performed continually)

- Project may have difficulty with leveling if you have used resource profiling (varying percentage availability)

- Manual adjustments can be made by allocating more resources to a task, rescheduling or splitting a task, reallocating tasks to a different resource, or overtime working

- Task constraints can be applied manually or through the leveling process and they determine when a task can or must start or finish

- Constraints can be applied on the advanced tab of the task information dialog box, or by setting the start or end date of a task

- Project will flag a constraint conflict if a constraint you are trying to apply can or will have an impact on another task

- Tasks with a constraint will have a constraint symbol in their task information box or details of all constraints can be displayed by applying the constraints dates table

- By default, Project re-calculates and re-schedules every time you make a change to a project, but this can be turned off in Project Options and the project will only be scheduled when you select Calculate Project from the Project ribbon

- Move Project allows you to change the project start data and re-schedule the whole project. It is also useful if you want to use an old project as a template for a new one. However, anomalies can creep in and it is still important to check the whole project

12 Viewing Data

Project holds a vast amount of information on your project and provides many options for selecting and viewing it. This chapter covers the different ways of viewing, grouping, filtering, sorting and displaying the information.

146 Views

147 Tables

148 Grouping

150 Fiscal Year

151 Filters

152 AutoFilter

153 Filter Criteria

154 Filter by Resource

155 Sorting

156 Highlight Filters

157 Background Highlighting

158 Custom Fields

159 Graphic Indicators

160 Summary

Views

In Project, views are the way that data is displayed for you to look at and work on. They can be placed into two main categories: task views and resource views. There are 20 task views and 7 resource views. You normally use task views when working with task information and resource views when working with resource information. The views can be further divided into sheets, charts, graphs and forms.

Sheets
Sheets (similar to spreadsheets) display information in rows and columns, with each task or resource being a row (horizontal) and each field in the task or resource being a column (vertical).

Charts and Graphs
Charts display graphical information in chart form, typical examples being the Gantt Chart and Network Diagram views. Graphs are used to display statistical information graphically in views, such as Resource Graph and Calendar.

Forms
Forms are used for the display and entry of detailed information on a task or resource.

Some views (such as Calendar) are simple, single views and some are compound views (such as Gantt Chart, which shows a sheet on the left and a chart on the right). You can also display a single view or two views (one above the other). The example below is a compound view with the Gantt Chart (table and chart) in the upper half and the Task Form in the lower half.

Tables

When working in a sheet view, there are a number of preset tables that can be used (applied) to access different types of information on tasks or resources. There are 17 task tables that can be applied to task views and 10 resource tables applicable to resource views.

If the view you have currently selected is not displaying quite the right information, you can apply a different table to change the view. The tasks or resources displayed remain the same but you will see different bits of information for them.

1 In Gantt chart view, select Task Usage from the View ribbon to replace the Task Entry view

	❶	Task Name	Work	Duration	Start	Details						Jul 11, '11	
1		− Initiation Stage	80 hrs	15 days	Fri 07/01/11	Work	8h	9.2h				11.6h	7.2h
2		− Agree Project Objectives	8 hrs	1 day	Fri 07/01/11	Work							
		Prudence Project	8 hrs		Fri 07/01/11	Work							
3		− Identify Stakeholders	8 hrs	1 day	Thu 07/07/11	Work	8h						
		Prudence Project	8 hrs		Thu 07/07/11	Work	8h						
4	🛈	− Select Project Team	32 hrs	4 days	Fri 07/08/11	Work		9.2h				11.6h	7.2h
	ᴀ	Prudence Project	16 hrs		Fri 07/08/11	Work		1.2h				3.6h	7.2h
		Bill Buggs	16 hrs		Fri 07/08/11	Work		8h				8h	
5	🖼	− Identify Business Case	16 hrs	2 days	Wed 07/13/11	Work							
		Bill Buggs	16 hrs		Wed 07/13/11	Work							

2 Then select Tables from the View ribbon and select Work from the built-in drop down list to show the work details

	Task Name	Work	Baseline	Variance	Actual	Details					Jul 11, '11
1	− Initiation Stage	80 hrs	80 hrs	0 hrs	0 hrs	Work	8h	9.2h			11.6h
2	− Agree Project Objectives	8 hrs	8 hrs	0 hrs	0 hrs	Work					
	Prudence Project	8 hrs	8 hrs	0 hrs	0 hrs	Work					
3	− Identify Stakeholders	8 hrs	8 hrs	0 hrs	0 hrs	Work	8h				
	Prudence Project	8 hrs	8 hrs	0 hrs	0 hrs	Work	8h				
4	− Select Project Team	32 hrs	32 hrs	0 hrs	0 hrs	Work		9.2h			11.6h
	Prudence Project	16 hrs	16 hrs	0 hrs	0 hrs	Work		1.2h			3.6h
	Bill Buggs	16 hrs	16 hrs	0 hrs	0 hrs	Work		8h			8h
5	− Identify Business Case	16 hrs	16 hrs	0 hrs	0 hrs	Work					
	Bill Buggs	16 hrs	16 hrs	0 hrs	0 hrs	Work					
6	− Risk Analysis	8 hrs	8 hrs	0 hrs	0 hrs	Work					
	Prudence Project	8 hrs	8 hrs	0 hrs	0 hrs	Work					
7	− Produce Outline Plan	8 hrs	8 hrs	0 hrs	0 hrs	Work					
	Prudence Project	8 hrs	8 hrs	0 hrs	0 hrs	Work					
8	Project Approval	0 hrs	0 hrs	0 hrs	0 hrs	Work					
9	− Strategy Stage	104 hrs	104 hrs	0 hrs	0 hrs	Work					
10	+ Interviews	32 hrs	32 hrs	0 hrs	0 hrs	Work					

3 Try applying the various different tables to the views that you use to see what is available

4 When you have finished, you can apply the default view back by selecting Gantt Chart from the View ribbon (the Table will automatically switch back to Entry)

Grouping

Grouping allows you to view your project tasks or resources grouped by any defined criteria. This can be applied to most, but not all, task and resource views. Each view has various standard groups to select from.

1 In Resource Sheet view, click the down arrow next to Group By on the View ribbon to get the drop-down list

2 Select Resource Group in the drop-down list and the resource sheet is rearranged by resource within group, as in the following illustration

3 Try selecting the various other Group By options in the drop-down list

4 To return to the standard view, just select No Groups in the Group By options

5 In Gantt Chart view, click the down arrow next to Group By on the View ribbon to get the drop-down list and select Constraint Type (see the following example)

Following step 5 opposite, the tasks are now grouped under the constraint types, as illustrated below.

	ⓘ	Task Name	Duration	Start	1, '11	Jul 18, '11
					12 13 14 15 16 17	18 19 20 21 22 23
		⊞ Constraint Type: As Soon As Possible	20d	Fri		
		⊟ Constraint Type: Must Finish On	0.5d	Fri		
20		2.7.2 Present to Management	0.5 days	Fri 08		
		⊟ Constraint Type: Start No Earlier Than	2d	Wed		
5		1.4 Identify Business Case	2 days	Wed 07	Bill Buggs	
12		2.1.2 Interview Staff	2 days	Thu 07		Pr

This is a useful view to see which constraints you have set on which tasks. The Summary Tasks group behaves in the same way as the normal summary tasks, and the view can be expanded and contracted by clicking the small plus or minus sign beside the group name.

The other useful feature is that Project rolls up totals by these groupings for you, useful for monitoring costs and work effort.

6 In Gantt chart view, select Group By>Critical from the View ribbon to apply this new grouping to the Gantt chart view

7 Next select Tables from the View ribbon and Work from the drop down list to display the rolled-up work effort totals on the critical and non-critical summary lines

Task Name	Work	Baseline	Jul 04, '11 ... Aug 01, '11
⊟ Critical No	336 hrs	336 hrs	
4	1.3 Select Project Team	24 hrs	24 hrs	Bill Buggs[50%],Prudence Project
5	1.4 Identify Business Case	16 hrs	16 hrs	Prudence Project
6	1.5 Risk Analysis	8 hrs	8 hrs	Prudence Project
7	1.6 Produce Outline Plan	8 hrs	8 hrs	Prudence Project
8	1.7 Project Approval	40 hrs	40 hrs	Prudence Project
12	2.1.2 Interview Staff	16 hrs	16 hrs	Prudence Project
11	2.1.1 Interview Managers	16 hrs	16 hrs	Prudence Project,Travel[$200.00]
13	2.2 Draft Requirements	16 hrs	16 hrs	Prudence Project
14	2.3 Feedback Sessions	16 hrs	16 hrs	Prudence Proje
15	2.4 Finalize Requirements	16 hrs	16 hrs	Prudenc
16	2.5 Review Risks	8 hrs	8 hrs	
17	2.6 Forward Plan	32 hrs	32 hrs	
19	2.7.1 Prepare Report	0 hrs	0 hrs	
21	2.8 Contingency	0 hrs	0 hrs	
23	3.1 Agree Requirements	40 hrs	40 hrs	
24	3.2 Select Software Packag	40 hrs	40 hrs	
25	3.3 Purchase Software	40 hrs	40 hrs	
26	3.4 Contingency	0 hrs	0 hrs	
28	4.1 Design Work	0 hrs	0 hrs	
29	4.2 Initial Build Work	0 hrs	0 hrs	
30	4.3 Dummy Task	0 hrs	0 hrs	
32	5.1 Train Users	0 hrs	0 hrs	
⊟ Critical Yes	16 hrs	16 hrs	
2	1.1 Agree Project Objectiv	8 hrs	8 hrs	Prudence Project
3	1.2 Identify Stakeholders	8 hrs	8 hrs	Prudence Project

8 Now try out the other Group By options on the Gantt chart and also take a look at the group by options on the other views

Hot tip

Note: the constraint type As Soon As Possible has been closed up in this illustration, as this is the default and not really a constraint.

Hot tip

In addition to the 12 predefined task and 6 predefined resource groupings, you can also create your own new groupings.

Fiscal Year

Project allows you to set the use of the fiscal year for the top, middle or bottom tier timescale. The following example shows how this can be used when the fiscal (business) year is different from the calendar year.

1 Select Project Options from the File ribbon and then select the Schedule option on the left hand side

2 Change Fiscal year starts in: to April, select Use starting year for FY numbering and click OK to close the Project Options dialog box

3 Select the down arrow beneath Timescale on the View ribbon and select Timescale from the drop down list to open the Timescale dialog box

4 On the Middle Tier, set Units to Years and deselect Use fiscal year. On the Bottom Tier set Units to Quarters, Use fiscal year and click OK.

The major timescale now displays calendar years and the minor scale displays fiscal quarters (as below)

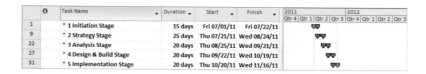

	0	Task Name	Duration	Start	Finish	2011				2012		
						Qtr 4	Qtr 1	Qtr 2	Qtr 3	Qtr 4	Qtr 1	Qtr 2	Qtr 3
1		+ 1 Initiation Stage	15 days	Fri 07/01/11	Fri 07/22/11		▽▽					
9		+ 2 Strategy Stage	25 days	Thu 07/21/11	Wed 08/24/11		▽▽					
22		+ 3 Analysis Stage	20 days	Thu 08/25/11	Wed 09/21/11		▽▽					
27		+ 4 Design & Build Stage	20 days	Thu 09/22/11	Wed 10/19/11		▽▽					
31		+ 5 Implementation Stage	20 days	Thu 10/20/11	Wed 11/16/11		▽▽					

Filters

In addition to its other selection capabilities, Project also allows you to filter and sort data before viewing (or printing). Filtering allows you to select just the information you wish to be displayed.

Predefined Filters

There are a number of predefined filters you can use to select things, such as late tasks, tasks in progress, work that is over budget, and so on. Project contains 33 predefined task filters and 24 predefined resource filters. In addition to these, you can also create your own custom filters to meet any specific requirements.

Filters can be used to focus on certain tasks in your project or on specific resources in the project. When you apply a filter, only the tasks or resources that meet the filter criteria are displayed. All other tasks and resources are hidden while you are using a filter.

Applying filters to your project does not change the data in any way, it just changes the way it is displayed.

AutoFilter

Project contains an AutoFilter feature that gives you a quick way of finding particular information in a field. When it's turned on, each column heading has an arrow on the right-hand side that can be used to apply a filter to the information in that column. You can apply filters to as many columns as you like and, once a filter has been applied to a column, a filter symbol will appear next to the column title (see illustration on page 152).

Interactive Filters

As well as specific filters, you can apply interactive filters that display a dialog box during the filtering process. You then provide the information to the dialog box to allow Project to complete the filtering process.

Custom Filters

If none of the predefined filters meet your requirements, you can define a new custom filter that exactly matches your needs. You can copy an existing filter and then edit it to meet your needs or you can create a completely new filter. The Filter Definition dialog box provides shortcuts to simplify this process.

Examples of these filters are given in the next few topics.

AutoFilter

When AutoFilter is turned on, you can apply filters to any column. The Select All and Clear All Filters options will remove any filter criteria, and the Filters>Custom option allows a column to be filtered by more than one criterion. The following example will demonstrate filtering on task duration.

 In Gantt chart view, Select Filter from the View ribbon and select Display Auto Filter from the drop down list to display the filter down arrows in each column header

Select Tables from the View ribbon and select Usage from the drop down list to apply the usage table

Task Name	Work	Duration	Start	Finish
− 1 Initiation Stage	80 hrs	15 days	Fri 07/01/11	Fri 07/22/11
1.3 Select Project Team	32 hrs	4 days	Fri 07/08/11	Ned 07/13/11
1.4 Identify Business Case	16 hrs	2 days	Ned 07/13/11	Thu 07/14/11
1.7 Project Approval	0 hrs	5 days	Mon 07/18/11	Fri 07/22/11
− 2 Strategy Stage	104 hrs	25 days	Thu 07/21/11	Ned 08/24/11
− 2.1 Interviews	32 hrs	6 days	Thu 07/21/11	Thu 07/28/11
2.1.1 Interview Manager:	16 hrs	2 days	Mon 07/25/11	Thu 07/28/11
2.1.2 Interview Staff	16 hrs	2 days	Thu 07/21/11	Fri 07/22/11
2.2 Draft Requirements	16 hrs	2 days	Fri 07/29/11	Mon 08/01/11
2.4 Finalize Requirements	0 hrs	2 days	Ned 08/03/11	Thu 08/04/11
2.6 Forward Plan	32 hrs	2 days	Mon 08/08/11	Tue 08/09/11

Click the Duration down arrow, select Filters, Greater than and then "is greater than" and "1 day" in the Custom Auto Filter dialog box. Note the filter symbol in the Duration column heading, indicating a filter has been applied to the data, as illustrated above

Change the Duration filter back to Select All then click the Work down arrow and select Filters>Custom

Select the required filters from the drop down list and click OK. Click AutoFilter again to turn them off

152

Filter Criteria

You can specify filter criteria interactively if you often need to make similar enquiries but with slightly different parameters. This is preferable to creating a large number of custom filters.

For example, you might want to get details of all tasks that are scheduled during the summer, to check for any vacation implications.

1 Select Other Views>More Views>Task Sheet from the View ribbon and click Apply, then select Tables>Schedule

2 Select Filter>Date Range from the View ribbon to open the Date Range dialog box

3 Enter or select the From date and click OK

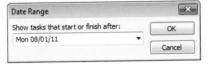

4 Enter or select the To date and click OK to display only the tasks in the selected range

	Task Name	Start	Finish	Late Start	Late Finish
9	− Strategy Stage	Thu 07/21/11	Wed 08/24/11	Tue 07/26/11	Wed 08/24/11
14	Feedback Sessions	Tue 08/02/11	Tue 08/02/11	Wed 08/03/11	Thu 08/04/11
15	Finalize Requirements	Wed 08/03/11	Thu 08/04/11	Thu 08/04/11	Mon 08/08/11
16	Review Risks	Fri 08/05/11	Fri 08/05/11	Mon 08/08/11	Tue 08/09/11
17	Forward Plan	Mon 08/08/11	Tue 08/09/11	Tue 08/09/11	Thu 08/11/11
18	− Report to Management	Wed 08/10/11	Fri 08/12/11	Thu 08/11/11	Fri 08/12/11
19	Prepare Report	Wed 08/10/11	Wed 08/10/11	Thu 08/11/11	Thu 08/11/11
20	Present to Management	Fri 08/12/11	Fri 08/12/11	Fri 08/12/11	Fri 08/12/11
21	Contingency	Mon 08/15/11	Wed 08/24/11	Mon 08/15/11	Wed 08/24/11
22	− Analysis Stage	Thu 08/25/11	Wed 09/21/11	Thu 08/25/11	Wed 09/21/11
23	Agree Requirements	Thu 08/25/11	Wed 08/31/11	Thu 08/25/11	Wed 08/31/11

In the example above, we selected the whole of August. Any task that is in progress during August is displayed, including tasks that start before August or end after August.

5 Select the Filter down arrow on the View ribbon and select No Filter from the drop down list to remove any filters applied

Filter by Resource

You can use resource filters in a Task view to display all tasks assigned to a resource. In a Resource view, you can use resource filters to select resources by Group.

1 In Gantt Chart view, click the Filter down arrow on the View ribbon and select Using Resource... (the three dots indicate further choices)

2 Click the down arrow, select the resource name (as illustrated) and click OK

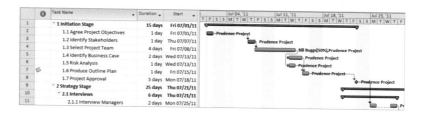

Note that, in the above example, all tasks assigned to the selected resource will be displayed (including tasks with additional resources assigned). The next example will filter by resource group in a resource view.

3 In Resource Sheet view, click the Filter down arrow on the View ribbon and select Group...

4 Type in the name of the group and click OK to filter by the resource group

Note that there is no selection facility on the Group dialog box in Step 4 above, you have to type in the group name correctly. Select the default No Filter from the Filter down arrow to remove any applied filters again.

Sorting

Tasks and Resources are usually displayed in ascending ID Number sequence. However, you can sort the display by any field or a combination of fields by specifying sort keys.

The following example will identify the largest pieces of work by sorting the tasks by summary task and then tasks in descending duration sequence.

1   In Task Sheet view, select Outline>All Subtasks from the View ribbon and then select Tables >Usage

2   Select Sort>Sort By from View ribbon to open the Sort dialog box, as illustrated below

3   Click on the Sort by down arrow, select Summary and select Descending, as illustrated right

4   Click on the Then by down arrow, select Duration and Descending, as illustrated above right

5   Uncheck Keep outline structure and click the Sort button to sort the tasks into the desired sequence, as illustrated below

	🛈	Task Name	Work	Duration	Start	Finish
9		⁻ 2 Strategy Stage	136 hrs	25 days	Thu 07/21/11	Wed 08/24/11
22		⁻ 3 Analysis Stage	120 hrs	20 days	Thu 08/25/11	Wed 09/21/11
1		⁻ 1 Initiation Stage	112 hrs	15 days	Fri 07/01/11	Fri 07/22/11
10		⁻ 2.1 Interviews	32 hrs	6 days	Thu 07/21/11	Thu 07/28/11
18	ⁱ	⁻ 2.7 Report to Management	16 hrs	2 days	Thu 08/11/11	Fri 08/12/11
8		1.7 Project Approval	40 hrs	5 days	Mon 07/18/11	Fri 07/22/11
23	ⁱ	3.1 Agree Requirements	40 hrs	5 days	Thu 08/25/11	Wed 08/31/11
24		3.2 Select Software Package	40 hrs	5 days	Thu 09/01/11	Wed 09/07/11
25		3.3 Purchase Software	40 hrs	5 days	Thu 09/08/11	Wed 09/14/11
4		1.3 Select Project Team	24 hrs	4 days	Fri 07/08/11	Wed 07/13/11
13		2.2 Draft Requirements	16 hrs	3 days	Fri 07/29/11	Tue 08/02/11
5		1.4 Identify Business Case	16 hrs	2 days	Wed 07/13/11	Thu 07/14/11
11		2.1.1 Interview Managers	16 hrs	2 days	Mon 07/25/11	Thu 07/28/11
12	▦	2.1.2 Interview Staff	16 hrs	2 days	Thu 07/21/11	Fri 07/22/11

Hot tip

Combining sorting with filters gives you a powerful range of features for viewing your data.

Highlight Filters

When Tasks and Resources are filtered, those that do not meet the filter criteria are hidden from view. Highlight filters can be used so that all tasks or resources remain visible, but the tasks or resources that meet the filter criteria are highlighted.

1 In Gantt Chart view, select Outline>All subtasks from the View ribbon and select Filter>More Filters from the View ribbon to open the More Filters dialog box

2 Select the required filter criteria (Resource Group in this example) and click the Highlight button

3 The Resource Group dialog box will open, type in the name of the resource group to be filtered and click OK

The resources belonging to the selected resource group will be highlighted in yellow, as in the following example.

4 Click the Filter down arrow on the View ribbon and select No Filter to return the display to normal again

Fonts and Highlighting

The Font group of functions allows you to change the font characteristics of text (font, style, size and text color) and also the background color and pattern of cells or rows, to convey additional meaning to the data. For example, we may wish to highlight certain problem tasks in a report to management.

1 In Gantt Chart view, select the task you wish to highlight by clicking in the Task ID (to select the whole task) and select the link in the bottom right of the Font group on the Task ribbon to open the Font dialog box

2 Select the down arrow beside Background Color: and select the desired color from the drop-down list

3 Select Background Pattern and click OK

As well as applying background highlighting, the Font dialog box allows you to edit the font characteristics. There are also individual functions in the Font group for most characteristics, such as bold and size. This gives significant scope for highlighting

Hot tip

If you select a dark background color, it will improve readability if you change the font to a light color.

Custom Fields

Project allows you to define, store and manipulate custom data, set up lists of acceptable values to make data entry more accurate, set formulae to perform calculations on the data and use graphic indicators to represent data. In the following example, we will set up a custom field to contain task risks.

1 In Gantt Chart view, select Custom Fields from the Project ribbon

2 Select Text for the Type (as illustrated) and click the Rename button

3 In the Rename Field dialog box type in the name (Risk)

4 Now click Lookup, enter the values (High, Medium, Low and None), select a default (None), click Close and click OK

5 Right-click on the heading of the Start column and select Insert Column

6 Scroll down to find the new field Text1 (Risk) and select it

7 Now type in or select the risk for each task (any new tasks created will be allocated the default None)

Graphic Indicators

In the previous topic, we set up a Custom field for risk and inserted a new column into the Gantt chart Entry table for it. We can now allocate a graphic indicator (traffic signal) to the risk field for visual impact.

1 In Gantt Chart view, right-click on the column heading of the relevant field (Risk) and select Custom Fields to open the Custom Fields dialog box (as illustrated opposite)

2 Click the Graphic Indicators button to open the Graphic Indicators dialog box

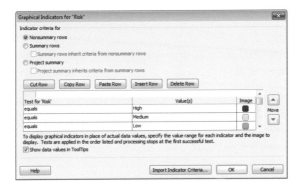

3 Using the drop-down arrows, select Test for Risk "equals", Value "High" and Image "red stop light" as above

4 Repeat for the other three values (Medium, Low and None), using appropriate yellow, green and white images

5 Click OK twice and your risks will now be graphic

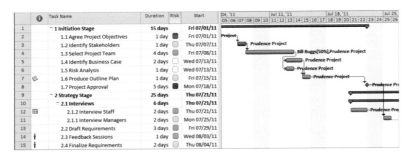

Summary

- Views are the ways that Project displays data on the screen; they consist of sheets (like spreadsheets), charts and graphs (visual) and forms (for detailed data entry)

- When working in a sheet view, there are a number of different tables that can be applied to vary the data in the sheet

- Grouping allows you to group the data by resource and various other options

- Fiscal year allows you to work with a non-calendar year

- Filters enable you to select which tasks or resources are displayed, according to selection criteria

- AutoFilter enables you to select a filter on one or more columns

- Filter criteria allow you to specify more complex filters based on ranges or comparisons

- Tasks and resources can be filtered by resource or resource group

- In addition to filtering, sorting allows the sequence in which tasks or other data are displayed to be defined, using up to three parameters

- Highlight filters allow all data to remain visible but with the data that meets the filter criteria being highlighted in yellow

- Background cell highlighting allows cells or rows to be highlighted in various colors independent of the data, for information purposes

- In addition to the background highlighting, the fonts can also be varied, as required

- Custom Fields allow you to define, store and manipulate custom data, set up lists of values to validate data entry and perform calculations on your data

- You can add custom fields into existing tables or create new tables containing them

- Graphic Indicators allow you to select appropriate images (such as traffic signals) to replace data values

13 Reports

This chapter covers the setup, preview and printing of charts and reports. It deals with visual reports, the useful copy picture function and some of the enhanced features introduced in Project 2010.

162 Printing a View

163 Headers and Footers

164 Previewing Reports

165 Page Setup and Scaling

166 Printing Reports

167 Visual Reports

168 Copy Picture

169 Project Collaboration

170 Enhanced Copy/Paste

172 Summary

Printing a View

Any chart or table view can be printed using the print function on the File ribbon. However, it is worthwhile setting the view up correctly before you print it.

1 To print a Gantt chart view, first format the screen to show the information you want to appear on the print by showing the appropriate level of subtasks (in the example below this is Outline Level 1)

2 Then move the vertical divider to cover or expose any fields on the table (left-hand panel)

3 Zoom in, out or to entire project (as illustrated below) to get the required view on the Gantt chart

4 Click Print on the File ribbon to print the view

5 To print a Resource sheet view, format the screen to show the information you wish to print by adjusting the scroll bars and the right-hand side of the screen

6 To hide any columns in the middle of the screen, right-click on the column header and select Hide column

7 Click Print on the File ribbon to print the view

Headers and Footers

In addition to the basic information displayed in a report, Project allows you to create your own headers (displayed at the top of each page) and footers (displayed at the bottom of each page). These are defined in the Page Setup dialog box.

You can enter any text you like and also include general system information, such as page number, date, project title, etc. You also have access to a wide range of project-level information.

1 Select Print from the File ribbon and then click on Page Setup to open the Page Setup dialog box

2 Select the Header tab at the top of the dialog box and the required Alignment tab in the center of the dialog box

3 Select the required information from the General and Project field drop down lists (in the example we have selected Company Name and Project Title) and click the Add button

4 Select the Footer tab and add any required information (in the example we have added "of" and the Total Page Count)

5 Click the OK button to save the header and footer information

6 Click the Print button or use print preview (next topic)

Previewing Reports

With Project, it is always a good idea to preview a report before printing it. That way you can make sure it will look the way you want it to and let you make any final adjustments to it. It may also save you wasting a lot of paper.

1 Open your project file in Gantt chart view, Show all subtasks and zoom in to days within weeks view

2 Select Print on the File ribbon to open the Print and Print Preview screen, as illustrated below

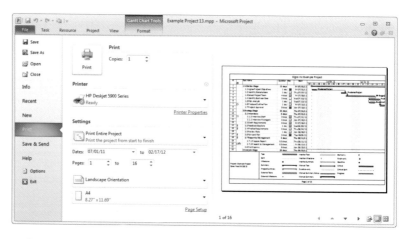

3 You can zoom the view in and out by clicking with your cursor (magnifying glass symbol) over the preview page on the right

4 Click the Multiple Pages button (bottom right-hand corner of the screen) to show the complete printout

Hot tip

Viewing multiple pages can save you from wasting a lot of paper.

Page Setup and Scaling

In addition to Preview, Print on the File ribbon also gives you some options: number of copies, printer, settings, orientation and paper size. It also has a link to Page Setup.

1 Select Print from the File ribbon and click the Page Setup link (underneath the Page Settings) to open the Page Setup dialog box

2 Select the Page tab, then scale by changing the Adjust to: percentage or select Fit to: and specify the number of pages wide and tall

3 Click OK to see the Print Preview

Hot tip

The preview illustrated on the left is the same report as illustrated at the foot of the page opposite, but scaled to fit on a single page.

4 From the print preview, click the Page Setup link to return to the page setup dialog box to make further adjustments or click Print when happy

In the page setup dialog box, you can also set page orientation (portrait or landscape); paper size (letter, A4, etc.); starting page number; margins and borders; legend information (displayed in the lower part of the screen, see preview illustration opposite) and whether to repeat on each page. You can also set various other view options, such as information to repeat on all pages, printing notes, printing blank pages, etc.

Printing Reports

There are 29 predefined report formats, in 6 groups, available in Project. The sixth group is also a custom group, where you can create your own report formats, either based on an existing report format or starting from new with a blank report.

1 Select Reports from the Project ribbon to open the Reports dialog box

2 Click on the required report group (such as Current Activities) and click Select to open the reports group dialog box

3 Click on the required report (such as Unstarted Tasks) and click Edit to open the Task Report dialog box

4 Change any information on the Definition, Details or Sort tabs

5 Click the Text button to edit the font details

6 Click OK to return to the above reports group dialog box (as after Step 2)

7 Click Select to preview the report in Print on the File ribbon and to print it

Visual Reports

Visual reports allows you to view your project data in Pivot Table reports in Microsoft Office Excel or Pivot Diagram views in Microsoft Office Visio Professional. There are several Excel and Visio templates provided with Project. These can also be edited, or you can create your own templates. As an example, we will create a budget cost report from a template for display in Excel.

1 In Gantt chart view, select Visual Reports from the Project ribbon to open the Visual Report Create Report dialog box, as illustrated below right

2 To limit the number of templates displayed, check or uncheck the Excel and Visio check boxes at the top and select the category of report from the six category tabs

3 Select the report template you wish to use (e.g. Budget Cost Report), click Edit Template to add or remove any required fields, then click View to display the report in the target application (the illustration below is an example of a budget cost report in an Excel Pivot Table)

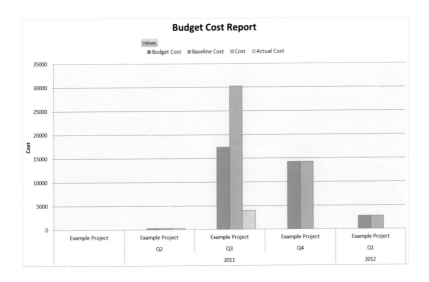

Copy Picture

The Copy Picture facility in Project is useful for including information, such as Gantt charts, in project reports. It can be selected from the down arrow next to Copy on the Task ribbon (Clipboard group) or from the Quick Access Toolbar.

1 First format your screen to show the information you require (in this example we are focusing on the work scheduled for the current month)

Don't forget

If you wish to add Copy Picture to the Quick Access Toolbar, it's covered on page 32.

2 Click Copy Picture on the Quick Access Toolbar or select from the Task ribbon to open the Copy Picture dialog box

3 Select Render image for screen or printer, as required, adjust the timescale, if required, and click OK

4 Open your target Office application (e.g. Word, PowerPoint, etc.) and paste the picture into the document in the required position, using the Edit>Paste or Paste Special from the Menu bar in that application (as in the example on the right)

Project Collaboration

Project 2010 introduces two enhancements that improve the options for project collaboration: SharePoint Synchronization and Enhanced Copy/Paste (covered in the next topic).

SharePoint Synchronization

With Project Professional 2010, you can now publish your project schedule to a SharePoint Foundation 2010 task list and receive task updates back from the resources they are allocated to. Project and SharePoint will synchronize the data. You can also share your project file by saving it to a SharePoint Foundation 2010 site.

Beware

Synchronization with SharePoint is not available in Project Standard 2010.

1 Open your project in Gantt chart view and select the appropriate table from the View ribbon

2 Select Save & Send from the File ribbon and select Save to SharePoint from the Share list

3 Browse for the SharePoint Server location and click Save

The other Share functions are:

- Sync with Tasks List: use this to synchronize the SharePoint task list and Project file following subsequent changes

- Save Project as File will save the full Project file to SharePoint for access by other team members

- Send as Attachment will email the full Project file to people who do not have access to SharePoint

Enhanced Copy/Paste

The Copy and Paste features now retain Project's outline levels and formatting information for sharing information between Project and other Office applications.

1 In Gantt chart view, select Timeline from the View ribbon to display the timeline in a split window

2 Select Copy Timeline (for email, presentation or full-size) from the Format ribbon, enter your target application and paste with format, as illustrated in PowerPoint below

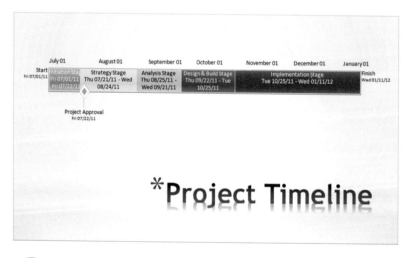

3 Once pasted into the target application, the whole image can be moved and re-sized in the normal way and each individual element of the image can also be edited

In a similar way, the timeline can be copied and pasted into Outlook and other office applications. Besides the timeline, any other elements of Project views can be copied and pasted.

As a further example, we will look at copying and pasting a task list from Project into Outlook.

1   In Gantt chart view, select the columns and rows you wish to copy (as illustrated below) and click Copy on the Task ribbon (Clipboard group)

2   Open your target application (Outlook in this example), create a new email message and paste with format

3   The pasted object can be positioned and re-sized, as required, and edited as a table (in the example illustrated above, the Predecessors column has been deleted and some of the column sizes have been adjusted for best view)

Summary

- Any chart or table view can be printed using the print function on the File ribbon, but it is worth spending a little time formatting the printout first

- Headers and footers can be defined using the page setup dialog box and can include system and project information, as well as any text information

- Before printing anything from Project, it is a very good idea to use print preview. Then the format and layout can be checked (and changed where necessary) before printing. It can also help to prevent wasting paper, as Project can generate quite a lot of empty or nearly empty pages

- Page setup can be used in Project in the normal way, to control the format (orientation, paper size, margins and legends) of a report

- Scaling can be used to reduce the number of pages that will be printed or to ensure that all the required information appears together on the same page

- In addition to being able to print from any view, there are 29 predefined reports that can be printed and also customized to provide just the information you want to see

- Visual reports allows data to be passed in a seamless manner between Project and Excel (as a pivot table) or Visio Professional (as a pivot diagram) for manipulation and display

- Copy picture allows a snapshot of the screen to be taken (with some editing options) for pasting into a document in another application, such as Word or PowerPoint

- Project collaboration has introduced enhanced features for sharing and synchronizing task lists and project files through SharePoint and by email

- Enhanced copy and paste allows graphic and text data to be passed to other office applications with formatting and outline information retained

- Once pasted into other office applications, the data can be edited and formatted for maximum impact

14 Tracking Progress

Once the project is underway, you need to update it with details of progress. This chapter covers the different types of progress information and how to deal with them.

174 Progress Tracking

175 Completed Work

176 Part Completed Work

177 Percentage Completed

178 Duration Completed

179 Entering Costs

180 Updating as Scheduled

181 Actual v Baseline

182 Tracking Gantt Chart

183 Budget Tracking

184 Project Statistics

185 Progress Lines

186 Summary

Progress Tracking

Once you have created your project plan and schedule, and the project has started, you can start tracking actual progress against the plan. You can enter information about progress on tasks by using actual start and finish dates, you can also input progress information on the percentage completed, actual and remaining duration, actual and remaining work, and actual and remaining cost. The most accurate way of tracking progress is by recording the actual work done and estimated work completion on each task. However, it is also the most time consuming so many people use the simpler percentage completed.

Depending on the type of information you input, Project will calculate the other relevant information. If you input a task finish date, Project will set the actual start date to the scheduled start date, and the actual duration to the difference between the start date and actual completion date.

Hot tip

Set a baseline before you start tracking progress and updating your project data.

Before you begin to enter actual information, complete your plan in as much detail as you are able, using contingency to allow for the unknown. Once you are happy with the plan, you can set a baseline and then start progress tracking.

Project stores information under three headings:

Baseline
The plan dates and task durations are stored when you set a baseline. These are then used to compare with the actual and scheduled dates.

Actual
Actual work that has taken place on tasks, which have been completed or part completed, and the date the work was started and completed.

Schedule
The planned dates and durations of tasks that have not yet been started or have been started but not yet completed.

As you enter your actual data, Project recalculates the schedule. So start with the earliest tasks on the schedule and work through. Once you have input all the actual information, and seen the impact on the schedule, you can re-evaluate the project and make any adjustments required to the project tasks to deal with any issues that have arisen.

Completed Work

Once a task has been completed, the easiest way to enter that information is by simply telling Project that the task is completed.

1 In Gantt chart view, click to select the completed task

2 Click the down arrow next to Mark On Track on the Task ribbon and select Update Tasks to open the Update Tasks dialog box, as illustrated below

3 Click the Actual Finish down arrow, select the finish date and click OK

4 If you open the Update Tasks dialog box again, you will see that the actual start date has also been set, the task is 100% complete and the remaining duration is now zero

5 Note also that a progress line has been drawn through the task, the task bar has turned blue (it is no longer on the critical path, as it has been completed) and a tick has been placed in the Task Information box

		Task Name	Duration	Start	Jul 04, '11 T F S S M T W T F S
1		⊟ **1 Initiation Stage**	**15 days**	**Fri 07/01/11**	
2	✓	1.1 Agree Project Objectives	1 day	Fri 07/01/11	Prudence Project
3		1.2 Identify Stakeholders	1 day	Thu 07/07/11	Pruc

6 Position your cursor over the Task Information box to display the date completed, as illustrated below

1		⊟ **1 Initiation Stage**	**15 days**	**Fri 07/01/11**	
2	✓	1.1 Agree Project Objectives	1 day	Fri 07/01/11	Prudence Project
3	✓ This task was completed on Fri 07/01/11.		1 day	Thu 07/07/11	Pruc
4		1.3 Select Project Team	4 days	Fri 07/08/11	

Part Completed Work

Where a number of days or hours of work have been carried out on a task, but the task is not yet fully completed, you can enter the actual work carried out.

 In Task Usage view, select Work Table from the View ribbon and select Work (planned) and Actual Work (carried out) from the Format ribbon

 Click in the Actual Work field of the resource for which you wish to enter the details, type the number of hours of actual work and press Enter

Note that the actual hours (5 hours in the above example) are rolled-up for the task. The work for the day is reduced to 5 hours and the remaining work (3 hours) is now scheduled on the following day. Project assumes that the time you have entered is "as at" the end of the day and carries forward any remaining work.

If the remaining work is now expected to take longer than the original estimate (3 hours in the example above), this can be entered by selecting the carried forward work field for the following day and entering whatever the new estimate to completion is

Hot tip

Actual work to date + estimate to completion is the most accurate way of tracking progress.

Percentage Completed

There is a certain amount of risk involved in using percentage completed as the measure of work done on a task. It is human nature for most people to be optimistic about their progress, so actual work to date plus estimated work to completion is usually more accurate. However, it will sometimes be appropriate to use percentage completed where it is not practical, to track work more closely.

1 Open your project in Task Sheet view, click Tables on the View ribbon and select Tracking from the drop down list

	Task Name	Act. Start	Act. Finish	% Comp.	Phys. % Comp.	Act. Dur.	Rem. Dur.	Act. Cost	Act. Work
1	⁻ Initiation Stage	Fri 07/01/11	NA	13%	0%	2 days	13.38 days	$520.00	13 hrs
2	Agree Project Objectives	Fri 07/01/11	Fri 07/01/11	100%	0%	1 day	0 days	$320.00	8 hrs
3	Identify Stakeholders	Thu 07/07/11	NA	73%	0%	1 day	0.38 days	$200.00	5 hrs
4	Select Project Team	NA	NA	0%	0%	0 days	4 days	$0.00	0 hrs
5	Identify Business Case	NA	NA	0%	0%	0 days	2 days	$0.00	0 hrs
6	Risk Analysis	NA	NA	0%	0%	0 days	1 day	$0.00	0 hrs
7	Produce Outline Plan	NA	NA	0%	0%	0 days	1 day	$0.00	0 hrs
8	Project Approval	NA	NA	0%	0%	0 days	5 days	$0.00	0 hrs

2 Update the percentage completed for tasks using the 25%, 50%, 75% functions on the Task ribbon, if appropriate, or use the Update Tasks function (from Mark on Track) to input any other percentages

3 Select Gantt Chart from the Task ribbon to switch back to Gantt chart view and note that the part completed tasks will have partial completion bars through them, as illustrated in the example below

	ⓘ	Task Name	Duration	Start	Jul 04, '11	Jul 11, '11	Jul 18, '11
1		⁻ 1 Initiation Stage	15.38 days	Fri 07/01/11			
2	✓	1.1 Agree Project Objectives	1 day	Fri 07/01/11	Prudence Project		
3	◆	1.2 Identify Stakeholders	1.38 days	Thu 07/07/11		Prudence Project	
4	⫯	1.3 Select Project Team	4 days	Fri 07/08/11		Bill Buggs[50%],Prudence Project	
5	⫯	1.4 Identify Business Case	2 days	Wed 07/13/11		Prudence Project	
6	⫯	1.5 Risk Analysis	1 day	Wed 07/13/11		Prudence Project	
7	✍	1.6 Produce Outline Plan	1 day	Fri 07/15/11		Prudence Project	
8		1.7 Project Approval	5 days	Mon 07/18/11			

Although the Tracking Table above gives you detailed control over progress, you can update tasks directly in Gantt chart view.

Duration Completed

You can enter the actual and remaining duration for a task in a similar way to the way you can enter actual work done.

1 In Gantt Chart view, select the task you want to enter duration information for

2 Select Update Tasks (from Mark on Track) on the Tasks ribbon to open the Update Tasks dialog box

3 Type in the actual duration to date, the remaining duration and click OK to update the task

4 Select Update Tasks again and note that Percentage complete and Actual start date have now been updated in line with the actual and remaining duration

As well as updating duration, the Update Tasks dialog box can also be used to update the percentage completed and the actual start and finish dates. Changes made to any of these fields will result in Project updating the other fields as appropriate, to keep the task details correct.

In the same way, the actual and remaining duration can also be edited directly in the Task Sheet Tracking view, as used in the Percentage Completed topic on the previous page. There are often several ways of doing the same thing in Project.

Entering Costs

Project will normally calculate costs for you based on the actual work involved in the task, and the cost details you entered for the resource assigned to the task. However, you can also enter actual cost details directly.

1 Select Options from the File ribbon, Schedule from the options list and scroll right down to the Calculation options

2 Clear the "Actual costs are always calculated by Project" check box and click OK

3 In Task Usage view, click Tables on the View ribbon and select Tracking from the drop down list

4 Select Cost and Actual Cost on the Format ribbon and de-select Work or any other details selected

5 Now select the Actual Cost field for the relevant task and resource and enter the actual cost (as illustrated below)

	Task Name	Fixed Cost	Fixed Cost Accrual	Total Cost	Details	Jul 25, '11				
11	⊟ Interview Managers	$0.00	Prorated	$482.50	Cost	$25.00	$37.50	$0.00	$262.50	$157.50
					Act. Cost	$25.00				
	Prudence Project			$320.00	Cost		$0.00	$0.00	$200.00	$120.00
					Act. Cost					
	Travel			$162.50	Cost	$25.00	$37.50	$0.00	$62.50	$37.50
					Act. Cost	$25.00				

While it is possible to enter all resource costs in this manner, it would become fairly time consuming. On the whole, it is far simpler to let Project calculate resource costs for you as you can vary the rate for different types of work (as covered in Variable Resource Costs, Cost Rate Tables and Applying Resource Rates in chapter 8).

Updating as Scheduled

If you have one or more tasks that have been started and/or completed in line with your schedule, you can use the Mark on Track function on the Task ribbon or Update Project dialog box from the Project ribbon.

1 In Gantt chart view, select Update Project from the Project ribbon

2 Select Update work as complete through, select the date you want all tasks updated to and click OK

3 If you receive a Planning Wizard warning that some unstarted tasks could not be rescheduled, click OK to continue, and update the Gantt chart (you can check the constraints on the relevant tasks later)

In the example above, the Gantt chart shows tasks 1.1 to 1.5 as fully complete and task 1.6 partially complete.

As can be seen in the Update Tasks dialog box (right), the task actually started on the working day before that selected at Step 2 (above). It is currently 63% complete and it is scheduled to be completed at the end of the day selected at step 2.

Actual v Baseline

Having set the project baseline, you can monitor your actual progress against this baseline at any time. The baseline and actual figures can be displayed in a number of tables and through the use of Tracking Gantt Chart view.

As an example, we will increase the actual work on a task and view the results.

1 In Gantt Chart view, select a task and use the Update Task dialog box to increase the actual and remaining duration

2 Click Tables on the View ribbon and select Work from the drop down list to open the Work Table

	Task Name	Work	Baseline	Variance	Actual	Remaining	% W. Comp.
1	− 1 Initiation Stage	128 hrs	112 hrs	16 hrs	85 hrs	43 hrs	66%
2	1.1 Agree Project Objectives	8 hrs	8 hrs	0 hrs	8 hrs	0 hrs	100%
3	1.2 Identify Stakeholders	8 hrs	8 hrs	0 hrs	8 hrs	0 hrs	100%
4	1.3 Select Project Team	24 hrs	24 hrs	0 hrs	24 hrs	0 hrs	100%
5	1.4 Identify Business Case	16 hrs	16 hrs	0 hrs	16 hrs	0 hrs	100%
6	1.5 Risk Analysis	16 hrs	8 hrs	8 hrs	16 hrs	0 hrs	100%
7	1.6 Produce Outline Plan	16 hrs	8 hrs	8 hrs	8 hrs	8 hrs	50%
8	1.7 Project Approval	40 hrs	40 hrs	0 hrs	5 hrs	35 hrs	13%

Hot tip

You can use the Filter on the Variance column to display non-zero values.

Note in Table View that Work = Actual + Remaining and that Variance = Work - Baseline.

Note also that, in the example above, we have used background cell highlighting to highlight the variances (this is not an automatic feature of Project).

3 Select the Cost table to display the actual and baseline cost and Variance table to see the start and finish date variance (as highlighted below)

	Task Name	Start	Finish	Baseline Start	Baseline Finish	Start Var.	Finish Var.
1	− 1 Initiation Stage	Fri 07/01/11	Mon 07/25/11	Fri 07/01/11	Fri 07/22/11	0 days	0.75 days
2	1.1 Agree Project Objectives	Fri 07/01/11	Fri 07/01/11	Fri 07/01/11	Fri 07/01/11	0 days	0 days
3	1.2 Identify Stakeholders	Thu 07/07/11	Fri 07/08/11	Thu 07/07/11	Thu 07/07/11	0 days	0.38 days
4	1.3 Select Project Team	Fri 07/08/11	Thu 07/14/11	Fri 07/08/11	Wed 07/13/11	0.38 days	0.38 days
5	1.4 Identify Business Case	Wed 07/13/11	Fri 07/15/11	Wed 07/13/11	Thu 07/14/11	0.38 days	0.38 days
6	1.5 Risk Analysis	Wed 07/13/11	Fri 07/15/11	Wed 07/13/11	Wed 07/13/11	0.38 days	1.38 days
7	1.6 Produce Outline Plan	Fri 07/15/11	Tue 07/19/11	Fri 07/15/11	Fri 07/15/11	0.38 days	1.38 days
8	1.7 Project Approval	Mon 07/18/11	Mon 07/25/11	Mon 07/18/11	Fri 07/22/11	0.38 days	0.75 days

Tracking Gantt Chart

The Tracking Gantt Chart view gives a graphical representation of the actual state of the project compared to the baseline.

 In Gantt chart view, select Tracking Gantt from the drop down list of views on the Task ribbon

Note that in the example above:

- Actual stage progress is shown as a hatched line below the stage summary bar at the top

- Percentage completed is displayed to the right of task bars and summary task bars

- The baseline task bars are displayed (black and white shaded) below the actual and schedule task bars

- Outline numbering does not appear in Tracking Gantt Chart view

- Completed tasks (actual) are displayed with a blue task bar

- Scheduled tasks (not yet started) are displayed with a red (if on the critical path) or blue (if not) task bar

- Started but not completed tasks are displayed with a red (if on the critical path) or blue (if not) part shaded task bar

- Baseline milestones are displayed as black and white diamonds

The project is currently one day behind schedule for the first milestone. However, there is a 5 day lag time between Producing the Outline Project Plan and the Project Approval milestone and we could, with the project sponsor's agreement, reduce this lag time to bring the project back on schedule.

Hot tip

Building in some lag time allows you to cope with task delays without ruining the schedule.

Budget Tracking

Project has some good facilities for cost and budget tracking.
The Cost resource type allows costs to be allocated for travel and
expenses, in addition to resource costs and fixed costs. Budgets
can also be assigned at the stage-level (summary task) or at the
project-level and tracked in more detail.

1 To review total costs for tasks, select Task Sheet view
from the drop down list on the Task ribbon

2 Click Tables on the View ribbon and select Cost from the
drop down list to display the total cost fields

	Task Name	Fixed Cost	Fixed Cost Accrual	Total Cost	Baseline	Variance	Actual	Remaining
1	= Initiation Stage	$0.00	Prorated	$1,952.00	$0.00	$1,952.00	$1,632.00	$320.00
2	Agree Project Objectives	$0.00	Prorated	$320.00	$0.00	$320.00	$320.00	$0.00
3	Identify Stakeholders	$0.00	Prorated	$0.00	$320.00	($320.00)	$0.00	$0.00
4	Select Project Team	$0.00	Prorated	$992.00	$1,440.00	($448.00)	$992.00	$0.00
5	Identify Business Case	$0.00	Prorated	$0.00	$960.00	($960.00)	$0.00	$0.00
6	Risk Analysis	$0.00	Prorated	$320.00	$320.00	$0.00	$320.00	$0.00
7	Produce Outline Plan	$0.00	Prorated	$320.00	$320.00	$0.00	$0.00	$320.00
8	Project Approval	$0.00	Prorated	$0.00	$0.00	$0.00	$0.00	$0.00

3 To review costs by resource, select Resource Sheet view,
click Tables on the View ribbon and select Cost, then
select Group By Resource Type on the View ribbon

	Resource Name	Cost	Baseline Cost	Variance	Actual Cost	Remaining
	⊟ Type: Work	$33,672.00	$13,580.00	$20,092.00	$1,632.00	$32,040.00
1	Prudence Project	$23,752.00	$10,140.00	$13,612.00	$832.00	$22,920.00
2	Joe Soap	$0.00	$0.00	$0.00	$0.00	$0.00
3	Mary Dee	$7,200.00	$0.00	$7,200.00	$0.00	$7,200.00
4	Wendy Page	$0.00	$0.00	$0.00	$0.00	$0.00
5	Bill Buggs	$2,720.00	$3,440.00	($720.00)	$800.00	$1,920.00
	⊟ Type: Material	$0.00	$0.00	$0.00	$0.00	$0.00
6	Paint	$0.00	$0.00	$0.00	$0.00	$0.00
7	Carpet	$0.00	$0.00	$0.00	$0.00	$0.00
	⊟ Type: Cost	$187.50	$200.00	($12.50)	$50.00	$137.50
8	Travel	$187.50	$200.00	($12.50)	$50.00	$137.50
9	Accomodation	$0.00	$0.00	$0.00	$0.00	$0.00
10	Training	$0.00	$0.00	$0.00	$0.00	$0.00

4 To review stage costs, select Task Sheet view and Show
Outline Level 1 and to add the project total select Project
Summary Task from the from the Format ribbon

	Task Name	Fixed Cost	Fixed Cost Accrual	Total Cost	Baseline	Variance	Actual	Remaining
0	= Example Project	$0.00	Prorated	$43,859.50	$0.00	$43,859.50	$1,682.00	$42,177.50
1	+ Initiation Stage	$0.00	Prorated	$1,952.00	$0.00	$1,952.00	$1,632.00	$320.00
9	+ Strategy Stage	$0.00	Prorated	$6,907.50	$0.00	$6,907.50	$50.00	$6,857.50
22	+ Analysis Stage	$0.00	Prorated	$17,000.00	$0.00	$17,000.00	$0.00	$17,000.00
27	+ Design & Build Stage	$0.00	Prorated	$6,600.00	$0.00	$6,600.00	$0.00	$6,600.00
31	+ Implementation Stage	$0.00	Prorated	$11,400.00	$0.00	$11,400.00	$0.00	$11,400.00

Project Statistics

The Project Statistics dialog box gives summary-level information for the whole project.

1 Select Project Information from the Project ribbon to open the Project Information dialog box

2 Click the Statistics button to open the Project Statistics dialog box (as illustrated below)

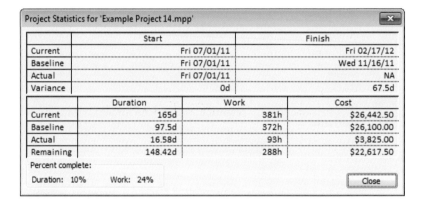

Project Statistics for 'Example Project 14.mpp'

	Start	Finish
Current	Fri 07/01/11	Fri 02/17/12
Baseline	Fri 07/01/11	Wed 11/16/11
Actual	Fri 07/01/11	NA
Variance	0d	67.5d

	Duration	Work	Cost
Current	165d	381h	$26,442.50
Baseline	97.5d	372h	$26,100.00
Actual	16.58d	93h	$3,825.00
Remaining	148.42d	288h	$22,617.50

Percent complete:
Duration: 10%   Work: 24%

Top Section

The top section of the Project Statistics dialog box shows the Current, Baseline and Actual Project Start and Finish Dates, together with the number of days Variance.

Middle Section

The middle section shows a summary of the Current, Baseline, Actual and Remaining Duration, Work and Cost. In the example above, duration, work and cost have all increased since the baseline was first set.

Bottom Section

Finally, the Percentage complete by Duration and Work is shown.

These project statistics are useful for a high-level snapshot report on the current status of the project.

Progress Lines

Progress Lines can be drawn on the Gantt Chart or Tracking Gantt Chart views at any date, to show the actual or expected progress as at that date.

They work by linking the tasks that are scheduled to be started, in progress or completed on that date. Tasks that are behind schedule result in peaks to the left of the line, while tasks that are ahead of schedule result in peaks to the right of the line.

1 In Gantt Chart or Tracking Gantt Chart view, click Gridlines on the Format ribbon and select Progress Lines from the drop down list

2 Select to display current progress line at the top, display progress in relation to the baseline at

the bottom right, and then click OK to show the progress line, as illustrated in the example below

In the example above, the progress line has been shown as at Monday, July 18 and at that date one task (Produce Outline Project Plan) was scheduled to be completed, but is not yet completed. Also the milestone Project Approval (to which we allocated a five day duration) is scheduled to have started but has not yet done so. On the Initiation Stage summary bar, the progress line is indicating that the stage is one day behind schedule.

Summary

- Once you have scheduled your project and allocated resources, you need to start tracking the actual progress of work on tasks against schedule

- If a task has been fully completed, you can mark it as completed by simply entering the finish date into the Update Tasks dialog box

- If a task is only part completed, work can be input as hours actually worked and estimated hours remaining to completion in Task Usage view

- The simplest way of inputting part completed work is to set the percentage complete in Task Sheet view, or use the percentage functions on the Task ribbon, but this is a less accurate method of tracking progress

- Duration completed and remaining duration can be input using the Update Tasks dialog box

- Actual costs of work completed can be entered in Task Usage view, but it is generally easier to allow Project to calculate the cost of work from the resource information

- Updating as scheduled is a quick way of entering progress information, if tasks are being completed more or less on schedule

- Having set a baseline, actual progress can be compared to baseline using the Work, Cost and Variance tables in Gantt Chart view

- Tracking Gantt Chart view gives you a view of actual and scheduled tasks superimposed over the baseline

- Budget tracking can be done by task or resource by applying the Cost table and, in summary, for stages and the complete project by showing the project summary task

- Project statistics gives you a summary view of current project progress against the baseline

- Finally, progress lines can add a visual indication of the state of the project at any point in time

Index

A

Actual	174
Actual Cost	31
Actual v Baseline	181
Actual Work	31
Adding Project Stages	65
Adding Structure	61
Allocating More Resources	136
All Subtasks (Show)	155
Applying a Contour	125
Applying Constraints	139
Applying Resource Rates	101
Assigning a Calendar	111
Assignment Information	31, 101
Assign Resources	24, 88, 91
Auto Filter	151, 152
Automatic Scheduling	23, 119
Auto Schedule	46
Available From	123

B

Background Color	22, 157
Backward Scheduling	129
Bar Styles	31
Base Calendar	84, 107
Baseline	26, 30, 174
Baseline Work	31
Budget Tracking	183

C

Calculate Project	26, 142
Calendars	105, 106
assigning a calendar	111
base calendars	106
holidays	109
new base calendar	110
project defaults	107, 108
resource calendar	106, 114
standard calendar	106, 109
task calendar	106, 112
Change Working Time	109, 114, 137
Change Working Week	115
Changing Dependencies	53

Changing the Timescale	66
Charts	146
Check Spelling	27
Clear Baseline	128
Clear Cell Content	23
Clear Cell Formatting	23
Clear Interim Plan	128
Clear Levelling	25
Column Settings	30
Column Width	47
Compare Projects	27
Completed Work	175
Conflicts	131
Constraint Conflicts	140
Constraint Dates	141
Constraints	74, 131
Constraint Type	148
Contingency	70
Contours	124
Copy	22
Copy Picture	168
Copy Timeline	93, 170
Cost	31
Cost Rate Tables	100
Cost Resources	86, 102
Create New Calendar	110
Critical	149
Critical Path	78
removing the critical path	82
Critical Tasks	30, 78, 79
Cumulative Work	31
Custom Auto Filter	152
Custom Fields	26, 30
Custom Filters	151
Customize Toolbar	32
Custom Reports	27

D

Date Range	153
Deadline Dates	76
Deadline Warning Indicator	76
Define Macro Security	29
Delete Note	75
Delete Task	55
Deliverables	38
Dependencies	74
Dependency Type	53, 74
Dependent Task	73
Details	56, 110

Display Auto Filter 152
Drawing 31
Duration 59, 119
Duration Completed 178

E

Edit Visual Basic 29
Effort Driven Scheduling 119, 121
Enhanced Collaboration 13
Enhanced Copy/Paste 170
Enhanced Tables 10
Entering Costs 179
Entire Project (View) 66
Existing Tasks 92

F

File 20
File Ribbon
    print 162
    project options 142
Fill 23
Filter 28, 152, 153, 154
    column 10
Find Text 23
Fiscal Year 150
Fixed Costs 96, 98
Fixed Duration Tasks 121
Fixed Unit Tasks 120
Fixed Work Tasks 122
Fix in Task Inspector 132
Font 157
Font Attributes 22
Fonts and Highlighting 157
Footer 163
Format 19, 30
Format Painter 22
Format Ribbon 30
    actual cost 179
    bar styles 30
    copy timeline 170
    cost 179
    drawings 31
    Gantt chart style 31
    project summary task 183
    show/hide 31
Formatting the Timeline 93

Forms 146
Forward Scheduling 119

G

Gantt Chart View 22, 28
Global Template 20
Go To Next Overallocation 25
Graphs 146
Gridlines 30, 185
    progress lines 185
Group 28, 84, 154
Group By 148

H

Header 163
Help 15, 21
Hide Column 162
Hide Window 29
Highlight 28, 156
Highlight Filters 156

I

Ignore Problems 132
Increase Duration 132
Indent 22, 63, 68, 70
Information Box 75, 113, 123, 141
Insert a Milestone 57
Insert Column 30
Insert Key 84
Insert Subproject 26
Insert Summary Task 63, 65
Insert Task 68, 118
Inspect 74
Interactive Filters 151
Interim Plans 26, 127

J

Justify 30

K

Key Deliverables	39
Key Tasks	39

L

Lag Time	72
Late Tasks	30
Layout	30
Lead Time	73
Level All	25
Leveling Options	25
Level Now	134
Level Resources	25, 134
Level Selection	25
Link	69
Link Tasks	22, 50, 51

M

Make Active	22
Make Inactive	22
Manual Adjustments	136
Manual Schedule	23, 47
Mark on Track	22, 175, 177
update tasks	178
Mark Task as Milestone	57
Material Costs	96
Material Resources	86
Max Units	84
Milestones	23, 38, 40, 57
Mode	23, 46, 118
More About Tasks	71
More Filters	156
More Views	22
Move Project	26, 143
Move Task	23, 54
Moving Around	77
Moving Linked Tasks	81
Multiple Resources	89

N

Navigation Ribbon	12
Network Diagram View	28
New Base Calendar	110
New Task	23, 49
New Window	29
Next Overallocation	133
Non-critical Tasks	78
Non Effort Driven Scheduling	121
Notes	31, 87

O

Options	20, 108
Outdent	22, 63, 70
Outline	28, 66, 155
Outline Numbering	31, 67
Outlook Address Book	25
Overallocated Resources	133
Overtime Rate	99
Overtime Working	137

P

Page Setup	163
Part Completed Work	176
Paste	22
PDF	12
Percentage Completed	177
Phases	62
Pivot Diagram	27, 167
Pivot Table	27, 167
Placeholder Text	12
Planning Wizard	81, 140, 180
Preceding Task	73
Predecessor Task	74
Predefined Filters	151
Predefined Reports	27
Print	21
Printing	162
Print Preview	21, 164
Progress Lines	185
Progress Tracking	174
actual	174
baseline	174
schedule	174

Project Calendars	105
Project Collaboration	169
Project Costs	95, 96
Project Defaults	107
Project Guide	17
assign resources	22
Project Information	20, 26, 134
Project Links	26
Project Management	9, 36
Project Milestones	40
Project Options	20, 107, 108, 142
Project Professional	13
Project Review	43
Project Ribbon	26
change working time	137
clear baseline	128
move project	143
project information	134
reports	166
set baseline	127
update project	180
visual reports	167
Project Scheduling	117
Project Server	20, 23, 24, 27
Project Stages	64, 70
Project Standard	12
Project Statistics	126, 184
Project Structure	62
Project Summary Task	31, 183
Project Timeline	92

Q

Quick Access Toolbar	18, 32
copy picture	168
customize toolbar	32

R

Reallocating Tasks	136
Recent Files	20
Recurring Tasks	58
Redo	32
Reduce Work	132
Re-link Tasks	81
Replace Text	23
Reports	27, 161, 166
Rescheduling a Task	136
Resource Allocation	134

Resource Availability Graph	88
Resource Calendar	107, 114
Resource Conflicts	132
Resource Contouring	123
Resource Costs	96, 97
Resource Deletion	84
Resource Details	25
Resource Group	148, 156
Resource ID	84
Resource Information	25, 85, 99, 111, 123
Resource Leveling Issues	135
Resource Leveling	134
Resource Notes	25, 87
Resource Pool	24
Resource Ribbon	24
next overallocation	133
resource allocation	134
Resources	38, 41, 83
cost	41, 86
material	41
work	41, 84
Resource Sheet	41, 84, 97, 123
Resource Usage	28
Respect Links	22
Revenue Costs	96

S

Save	32, 42
Save As	42
Save & Send	21
Save to SharePoint	169
Schedule	142, 153, 174
Schedule Options	108
Scheduling	117
automatic	11, 119
manual	11, 118
mode	118
user-controlled	11, 118
Scheduling Concerns	11
Scrollbars	77
Scroll to Task	23, 77
Selected Tasks	29
Set Baseline	26, 126, 127
SharePoint Synchronization	8, 13, 21, 169
Share Resources	24
Sheets	146
Show Ignored Problems	74
Show Suggestions	74
Show Warnings	74
Slack	30
Sliders	77

Slippage 30
SMART Objectives 37
Smart Tag 55
Sort 28
Sort By 28, 155
Spell Check 27
Split Task 22, 80
Splitting Tasks 80
Stages 62
Standard Calendar 109
Standard Rate 99
Start Date 26
Starting Year for FY Numbering 150
Statistics 128, 184
Status Date 27
Structured Approach 36
Styles 31
Substitute Resources 24
Subtasks 62, 63, 68
Summary Tasks 23, 31, 63, 70
Switch Windows 29
Synchronize 13, 21
Sync to Protected Actuals 27

T

Tables 28, 147, 149, 177
    applying tables 147
    cost 183
    cost table 98
    entry 147
    schedule 153
    tracking 177, 179
    usage 152, 155
    work 147, 149, 181
Task 22
Task Calendar 107, 112
Task Constraints 138
Task Contouring 124
Task Dependency 52, 53, 72, 73
Task Details 23
Task Duration 60
Task Form 56
Task Information 23, 113
Task Inspector 11, 23, 74
Task Name Field 46
Task Note 23, 75
Task Progress 22
Task Ribbon 22
    insert task 118
    mark on track 175, 177
    mode 118

    task sheet view 183
    update tasks 175
Tasks 38, 39
    active 12
    adding tasks 49
    changing dependencies 53
    creating a task 46
    delete 55
    dependant 50
    duration 48
    inactive 12
    linking 50
    link line 52
    move a task 54
    recurring task 58
    task dependencies 50
    task duration 48
    task ID 46
    task list 46
    task types 119
        fixed duration task 121
        fixed unit task 120
        fixed work task 122
    unlink 52
Task Sheet 153, 177, 183
Task Usage 101, 176, 179
Team Planner 13, 24, 90
Template 21
Text Styles 30
Text Wrap 10
Timeline 92
    add existing task 93
    annotations 93
    background color 93
    call out tasks 93
    font group 93
    text color 93
    text styles 93
Timeline View 11, 29
Timescale 29, 66, 150
Timescale dialog box 150
Tool Tips 12
Tracking 177
Tracking Gantt Chart 181, 182
Tracking Progress 173

U

Undo 32, 55
Units 119
Unlink Tasks 22, 52
Update Project 27, 180

191

Update Tasks 175
Updating as Scheduled 180
Usage 152
User Controlled Scheduling 118
User Interface 10, 17, 18, 34
  file tab 18
  format tab 19, 30
  project tab 19, 26
  quick access toolbar 18, 32
  resource tab 19, 24
  task tab 19
  view tab 19, 28
Using Cost Resources 103
Using Resource 154

V

Vacations and Absences 115
Variable Resource Costs 99
Version Comparison 12
View 28
View Entire Project 66
Viewing Constraints 141
Viewing Data 145
View Macros 29
View Ribbon 28
  details 120
  filter 152, 153, 154
  gridlines 185
  group by 148
  outline 155
  resource views 28
  table 141
  tables 147, 149, 152, 177, 183
  task sheet 153
  task views 28
Views 146
  charts 146
  forms 146
  graphs 146
  leveling Gantt chart 134
  resource allocation 134
  resource sheet 86
  resource usage 125
  task entry 147
  task sheet 177
  task usage 147, 176, 179
  tracking Gantt chart 181, 182
Visual Change Highlights 69
Visual Reports 27
  pivot diagram 167
  pivot table 167

W

Whole Project (View) 29
Work 31, 119, 149
Work Breakdown Structure 26, 62, 67, 70
Work Contour 125
Work Effort 59
Work Effort v Duration 59
Working with Tasks 45
Work Table 147, 181
Work Weeks 110
Wrap Text 30, 47, 67

Z

Zoom 29, 66
Zoom Custom 66
Zoom In 66
Zoom Out 66